Philosophy and

D0627780

To D. J. P.

Philosophy and the Mind

Jenny Teichman

Basil Blackwell

Copyright © Jenny Teichman 1988

First published 1988

Basil Blackwell Ltd
108 Cowley Road, Oxford, OX4 1JF, UK

Basil Blackwell Inc.
432 Park Avenue South, Suite 1503
New York, NY 10016, USA

All rights reserved. Except for the quotation of short passages for the purposes
of criticism and review, no part of this publication may be reproduced, stored in
a retrieval system or transmitted, in any form or by any means, electronic,
mechanical, photocopying, recording or otherwise, without the prior permission
of the publisher.

Except in the United States of America, this book is sold subject to the
condition that it shall not, by way of trade or otherwise, be lent, re-sold, hired
out, or otherwise circulated without the publisher's prior consent in any form of
binding or cover other than that in which it is published and without a similar
condition including this condition being imposed on the subsequent purchaser.

British Library Cataloguing in Publication Data

Teichman, Jenny.
  Philosophy and the mind.
  1. Mind — Philosophical perspectives.
  I. Title
  128' .2

  ISBN 0–631–15752–2
  ISBN 0–631–15753–0 Pbk

Library of Congress Cataloging in Publication Data

Teichman, Jenny.
  Philosophy and the mind/Jenny Teichman.
    p. cm.
  Bibliography: p.
  Includes index.
  ISBN 0–631–15752–0
  ISBN 0–631–15753–0 (pbk.).
  1. Psychology—Philosophy. I. Title.
BF38. T38 1988
128' .2—dc19

Typeset in 10½ on 11½ pt Times
by Photo·Graphics, Honiton, Devon
Printed in Great Britain by T.J. Press (Padstow) Ltd

LIBRARY
ALMA COLLEGE
ALMA, MICHIGAN

Contents

Introduction

This book is intended as an account of the main developments which have taken place in philosophical psychology, or the philosophy of mind, since about 1945. Its aim is to outline, explain and criticise the more significant recent theories in that field. Carrying out this aim has involved describing a number of modern writings in the philosophy of mind.

It is probably true to say that in the English-speaking world the two most prominent trends in philosophy of mind since 1945 have been materialism, which takes various forms, and the philosophy of linguistic analysis (so-called). It should be noted, however, that there is some overlap between them.

To some extent materialist philosophers like to see themselves as sharing the aim of science, which they perceive as a search leading to the discovery of general laws. Thus they seek wide and simple general accounts of the nature of the mind. Materialist theories are 'nothing but' theories. For instance, behaviourism is the theory that the mind is nothing but the body in action, and physicalism is the theory that mental events are nothing but brain events. In other words materialist theories are both *scientistic* and *reductive*.

If we conceive of linguistic philosophy as a kind of philosophy which broadly speaking has to do with language then it too takes more than one form. One variety consists of constructing theories about language, as Wittgenstein did in *Tractatus Logico-Philosophicus*. Another type takes the form of searching for a logical solution to a particular problem or set of problems. This kind of linguistic philosophy often leads to the recognition of previously unnoticed distinctions, and may involve inventing new logical terms, or even a whole new formal language, in order to adumbrate them. Russell's *Theory of Descriptions* is an example. And, finally, some linguistic philosophy seeks to solve problems by undertaking detailed but non-formal analyses of ordinary language. The so-called analytic method has been applied to a wide range of philosophical topics. Its application to philosophical psychology is the subject of Part II of this book.

It seems to me that the scientistic and reductive philosophical principles of materialism stem partly from Marxism, partly from logical positivism (especially the work of Rudolf Carnap), and partly from the dogmas of J. B. Watson, the American founder of behaviourism.

Linguistic philosophy too has roots in logical positivism, in so far as the Vienna Circle included Carnap and sometimes Ludwig Wittgenstein. Each of these men constructed influential philosophical theories about language. However, linguistic philosophy also has features which I believe can be traced to the influence of the Cambridge philosopher G. E. Moore. Moore's insistence on getting clear, or trying to get clear, about the meanings of one's words has strongly affected the style of twentieth-century philosophy, especially in Britain.

Contemporary English-speaking philosophy has had quite a few (mainlyEnglish-speaking) critics. These critics include philosophers, but most are professional academics working in speculative disciplines which lie not far from philosophy; they are for example sociologists or historians or political theorists.

One common general criticism of Anglo-American philosophy is that it is narrow, inward-looking and chauvinistic, not interested in European thought, and not interested in related disciplines.

As well as this general criticism the (mainly British) school of linguistic or analytic philosophy is sometimes singled out for special attacks. There is a blistering attack by Ernest Gellner, whose book *Words and Things* is very entertaining if you enjoy reading knockabout academic abuse. However it seems to me that his criticisms apply in the main to third-rate instances of linguistic philosophy, and not to subtle and illuminating writers such as Wittgenstein. Of course third-rate linguistic philosophy is no better than any other kind of third-rate stuff.

The more general claim, that British and American philosophy as a whole is narrow and chauvinistic, is to my mind quite probably true.

Part III of this book is devoted to two French philosophers, primarily on account of the inherent importance of their work, but also, and incidentally, in order to demonstrate that not all philosophy of mind is proceeding in Anglo-Saxon directions.

Materialism and the philosophy of linguistic analysis represent two different views on the relationship between philosophy and science. At the same time (as it seems to me), English and French philosophers have somewhat different presuppositions about which of the sciences, if any, are specially relevant to current philosophical concerns. For these two reasons there is some discussion in Part IV about the philosophy of science and about the autonomy of the special sciences.

The reader will here and there come across descriptions of strange imaginary states of affairs, and perhaps something should be said about these. The use in philosophy of real and imaginary examples has a long history which goes back to Socrates. The creators of the 'thought experiments' which are described in this book (mainly in Part I) intended them as descriptions of logically possible counter-examples to various positive and negative generalisations about the nature of the mind. They are intended, that is to say, to show either that something said to be possible is impossible, or that something said to be impossible is possible. From time to time I invent my own examples (or small 'thought-experiments') in order to develop a point. But I have tried to make it always clear who is talking when.

In so far as I have a theory of my own about the mind it is that knowledge is in some sense a pluralism. Explanation is pluralistic, the pluralism is ineradicable, reductive accounts of the nature of the mind must therefore be either false or incomplete. However the explication or defence of my own 'theory', if it deserves that name, is not to be thought of as an attempt to give a final answer to questions about the nature of the mind. 'Final answers' are usually dogmatic and weak.

The plan of the book is thematic, not chronological: the material could not be arranged chronologically, because the life-spans of the authors whose writings are described herein are roughly contemporaneous. Nevertheless I have tried to show how later theories have grown out of earlier ones when this is in fact the case. And readers should get some idea of chronology from the Appendix and from the Bibliography.

Part I
Materialism

1

Behaviourism

J. B. Watson is usually regarded as the founder of behaviourism. Watson (1878–1958) was an American psychologist who taught at Johns Hopkins University until 1920, after which he took up a career in advertising ('consumer research').

Watson was an extreme monistic materialist who began by rejecting introspection as a method of enquiry and then proceeded to deny the very existence of introspectible states. That is, he denied the existence of all such 'mentalistic' items as thoughts, emotions and beliefs. Watson proposed the theory that a thought is nothing but an incipient movement of the larynx and an emotion nothing but an internal pattern of bodily adjustment.

Watson as a psychologist conducted empirical research into the behaviour of rats, and this somehow led him to form a non-empirical general theory about the nature of the human mind. In 1928, after ceasing to work in empirical psychology, he wrote *The Psychological Care of the Child*, a book based not on research but rather on arbitrary a priori principles. In this book he advocated minimal affection and minimal contact in the upbringing of children.

What Is Behaviour?

There has been a lot of disagreement among behavioural psychologists about what is to count as behaviour. Strange to say, few if any modern philosophers interested themselves in this definitional question even during the years when the philosophy of linguistic analysis was greatly in favour.

In ordinary language the word 'behaviour' is not confined to the actions of human beings, nor even to the movements of living things in general. Ordinary language allows us to speak of the actions and reactions, the workings and the performance, in short the 'behaviour', of all kinds of objects and materials; for example, of acids and salts and metals; and organs and cells and other parts of living beings; and volcanoes and glaciers and continental plates; and motor cars and computers and other machines.

But of course the behaviour of behaviourism is human behaviour, or, more generally, animal behaviour.

Some of the things which people and other animals do are done with awareness, that is, consciously. Of these some are voluntary (for instance actions needed to obtain food), some are involuntary (like sneezing) and some can be either (like blinking and coughing).

Other things which people and animals do or undergo are done or undergone unconsciously. For example a normal healthy individual is not usually conscious of the process of digestion.

Voluntary actions are actions which one can oneself suppress. They are generally conscious, though some are *habitual* and therefore as it were semi-conscious. Reflex actions are involuntary but it is possible to be conscious of some (but not all) of them. For instance, one is normally conscious of the fact that one is sneezing.

Unlike voluntary action, reflex action does not necessarily involve the brain.

Which of these types of happening do behaviourists mean to refer to, when they speak of behaviour?

Generally speaking, contemporary philosophers appear to take 'behaviour' to refer to all publicly observable ordinary voluntary or involuntary acts of which the subject is normally but not invariably conscious – events like running, winking, talking, eating, grimacing and so on. Philosophers of a behaviouristic cast of mind do not necessarily deny the existence of consciousness, nor do they deny that there is a difference between voluntary and involuntary actions.

Experimental psychologists, on the other hand, generally include automatic happenings such as digestion and salivation, also all reflex actions, under the term 'behaviour'.

Some experimental psychologists accept behaviourism as a method without committing themselves to any philosophical theories as to the ultimate nature of the mind. Others, such as Watson, are far more radical; these deny the existence of mental events as such.

One might feel that it cannot be easy for anyone, even a behaviourist, to claim that there are no genuine differences between physiological happenings like digestion, of which the subject is not normally conscious, and normally cannot control; events like wincing and winking, which the subject or actor might or might not be aware of; and actions such as writing essays and experimenting with rats, which the actor is normally fully conscious of.

However even radical behaviourists in fact can accept that actions are either conscious and voluntary, or reflex. Thus according to the followers of B. F. Skinner the difference between 'so-called conscious action' and reflex action is that the latter is the result of evolution and the former the result of environment; in other words, the distinction has nothing to do with internal mental states. Internal mental states are fictions.

B. F. Skinner

The American psychologist B. F. Skinner is a radical behaviourist strongly influenced by the work of J. B. Watson. Like Watson he is by profession an experimental psychologist, and like Watson he has proposed a general philosophical theory about the nature of the mind.

Skinner writes 'I do not believe that there is a world of mentation [i.e. mental happenings] or subjective experience . . . thinking is simply behaving and may be analysed as such.'

It looks as if he is saying that he thinks there are no thoughts and believes there are no beliefs!

The reasons he adduces for this difficult position are as follows.

It is possible to give causal explanations of the laboratory behaviour of rats and other experimental animals without making any reference to the creatures' feelings and beliefs. Rat behaviour appears to consist of reflex actions, which can be explained in terms of genetic theory, and of actions which the rats have been trained to do, that is, which they have been induced to perform by external conditions such as pains and rewards. These external conditions can be imposed by a human experimenter, or they might instead just be part of the physical environment. Skinner thinks that human beings too are trained by undergoing the painful or pleasant consequences of their own actions, and indeed says that all human behaviour which is not part of the genetic endowment can ultimately be explained in terms of natural or social punishments and rewards.

Well, but doesn't the rat, or the human being, behave as it does because it associates pleasure (e.g. food) and pain with certain of its own actions, and also because it *wants* the food, and *fears* the pain, and so on? And surely making associative connections, and wanting, and fearing, are mental events? If the rat made no associations and had no wants or fears it would not learn, would it?

To this and similar objections Skinner has five answers, none of which seem any good to me. But readers must judge for themselves.

His first answer is

> All feelings, including fearing and wanting, are bodily, not mental.

Skinner gives no proof of this, apart from the suggestion that the word 'feeling' just *means* something bodily. Now this is a linguistic argument, and it won't work unless the linguistic facts are as Skinner asserts them to be. But if we look at the linguistic facts there is little evidence that the word 'feeling' invariably makes direct reference to locatable bodily events. For example it is unrealistic to insist that the sense of the word 'feel' in the sentence 'I feel that Skinner has made a mistake here' is such as to involve any direct reference to locatable bodily events.

Skinner's second answer is

> If internal mental non-bodily feelings did exist they would be much harder to identify than behaviour.

But this is only a methodological consideration and as such cannot prove that feelings don't exist.

His third answer is

> The animal does not make associations: the associations are made by the experimenter.

In the second part of this reply Skinner asserts the existence of the thing whose existence he denies in the first part. For what he here says is that, although when rats or human beings are being experimented on they have no interior mental life, the experimenters themselves *do* have a mental life. So at least *some* creatures have a mental life, namely, experimental psychologists. . . .

The fourth answer is

> Intentions, purposes and suchlike mental items are inventions.

Skinner says that it is only under experimental conditions that the causal connections between conditioning and behaviour become obvious. Environmental causes of human behaviour are rarely obvious. For this reason the concepts of intention, purpose, emotion and so on have been *invented* in a vain attempt to explain behaviour, in the same way that the ancient Greeks invented Zeus in a vain attempt to explain thunder.

Well, who invented these notions of intention, emotion, etc.? And what is it to invent a notion? Isn't the concept of inventing a notion at least as mentalistic, and therefore in Skinner's terms at least as vain and superfluous, as the notions of intention, emotion and purpose themselves? Try as he might, Skinner seems unable to escape from the mentalistic concepts he derides. Perhaps they are not so superfluous after all.

And the fifth answer is

All reference to mental items is pre-scientific [i.e. unscientific].

Using an unexamined notion of *the scientific*, Skinner says that virtually all thinkers before Newton were unscientific. He then accuses anti-behaviourists of being unscientific in the same way as he believes Aristotle to have been.

He remarks

> Aristotle argued that a falling body accelerated because it grew more jubilant as it found itself nearer home . . . later authorities supposed that a projectile was carried forward by an impetus, sometimes called an 'impetuosity'. All this was eventually abandoned, and to good effect, but the behavioural sciences still appeal to comparable internal states.

In other words, Skinner not only thinks that only scientific reasoning is valid, and not only sees no reason to examine the concept of the scientific, he also thinks that *personifying persons* is just as 'unscientific', just as unreasonable, as personifying inanimate objects.

Skinner's most important underpinning philosophical principle, implicit in all his work, is usually assumed rather than defended by him. However there is a brief statement of it in the first chapter of his book *Beyond Freedom and Dignity*. This significant principle, which possibly comes to Skinner from Hume, is that all genuine explanation has to refer to antecedent events and cannot refer to anything else.

If this quasi-Humean thesis were true I think it would indeed rule out the possibility of non-behaviourist psychology. It would also rule out philosophy, mathematics, all classificatory sciences and those sciences, such as genetics, which find out how things work. For questions about how things work cannot be answered in full simply by reference to antecedent events.

Gilbert Ryle

Ryle published his celebrated book *The Concept of Mind* in 1949. In this work Ryle stated that he was not defending behaviourism. Behaviourism, he said, is a method of research used by experimental psychologists, not a philosophical doctrine. In spite of this disclaimer Ryle is now widely regarded as an exponent of behaviourism. The reasons are not far to seek.

The scope of behaviourism has always extended beyond the methodology of psychology.

It is not only professional philosophers who hold philosophical theories. Psychologists in particular are much given to philosophical theorising. They are far more prone to this than are, say, zoologists, or physiologists. Indeed it is not uncommon for psychologists to advocate drastic general theories about all kinds of things – mind, philosophy, education, marriage, motherhood, politics and the reform of society through the application of the principles of psychology.

Behaviourism was indeed invented by psychologists but it is a philosophical theory for all that, and Ryle himself at least *appears* at times to be expounding it.

Whether or not Ryle is a behaviourist he is certainly a 'linguistic philosopher' in that he uses logic and facts about language to solve philosophical problems. For this reason I discuss Ryle in Part II rather than here, leaving the question as to his ultimate classification for future historians of philosophy to decide.

2

Physicalism

Physicalism and Behaviourism

The word 'physicalism' was coined by Rudolf Carnap as a synonym for 'behaviourism', and was later used by J. J. C. Smart in his book *Philosophy and Scientific Realism*. Smart shares some of Carnap's views, but he makes a distinction between behaviourism, which he perceives as a linguistic and chiefly Rylean enterprise, and physicalism, which he sees as more scientific and more sound than philosophical behaviourism.

Post-Carnapian (anti-behaviourist) physicalism was first pro-pounded by Smart and by D. M. Armstrong, at a time when linguistic analysis and Rylean behaviourism were the dominant trends in English and American philosophy. Because its first exponents were natives or residents of Australia, the theory was nicknamed 'the Australian heresy'.

Physicalism is also sometimes called *the identity theory* or *the contingent identity theory*, for reasons which will become clear below.

The physicalist view of the world, says Smart, comprises the view that 'the sciences of biology and psychology . . . are an application of physics and chemistry to natural history . . . [and] that organisms are simply very complicated physico-chemical mechanisms.' Smart believes that the sciences of physics and chemistry can 'encompass everything in the world'. Elsewhere he writes 'That *everything* should be explicable in terms of physics . . . except the occurrence of sensations seems to me to be frankly unbelievable' (my italics).

The arguments in favour of physicalism are both negative and positive. Negatively, physicalists attempt to prove that behaviourism is false or inadequate. Positively, they argue that only a scientific world-view can provide genuine explanations. Hence (they argue) any true explanations of the nature of mental phenomena will show that these phenomena can be identified with events of a kind which form the subject matter of some science. In all probability mental events are the very same things as brain events, the subject matter of the science of neuro-physiology.

Part of the attempted proof that mental events are the very same things as brain events takes the form of a theory about the nature of identity, a theory about the meaning or meanings of identity-statements. This theory about identity has been dubbed 'the contingent identity thesis'.

Arguments for Physicalism: Causation and Explanation

One argument against behaviourism runs as follows.

Everyone really thinks that human actions are explained in part by the human individuals' beliefs, intentions, sensations, etc. According to Skinnerian behaviourism, though, intentions, beliefs and so on are mere responses to stimuli; and according to Rylean behaviourism mental events are really only dispositions to act or ways of acting. In other words, if behaviourism is true, then intentions and beliefs are themselves only bits of actual or potential behaviour. But if an intention (say) is itself nothing except actual or potential behaviour, how can it *explain* behaviour? It seems impossible that the ultimate explanation of behaviour is only more and more behaviour. The correct analysis of the nature of beliefs, sensations and intentions must be of a kind which allows us to see how beliefs, sensations and intentions explain actions. Now, the physicalist analysis identifies beliefs and so on with brain states. Propositions about brain states have explanatory power, for they belong to the science of neuro-physiology, and neuro-physiology, according at least to Smart, is reducible to physics. And physics quite obviously has enormous explanatory power.

Still, although behaviour is not apt for explaining more behaviour, it does not immediately follow that physics and physiology are any more apt at producing the right kind of explanation. Physics and physiology explain many things, but they are relatively unapt for producing explanations of ordinary human behaviour. They are unapt in comparison with the explanations that are couched in the terminology of everyday 'folk psychology'. The concepts of mentality as these appear in ordinary commonsense discussions of ordinary people have more explanatory power, more predictive power, than the proposed analyses of those notions which are given to us by physicalism. For example, the fine-grained complexity of the concept of *belief*, described below, has not so far been mapped on to any set of physiological or physical statements.

Arguments for Physicalism: The Pre-eminence of Scientific Explanation

Many of us in the West believe that we live in a wholly physical universe, a universe which has no room for such items as spiritual substances. Most of us believe this on authoritarian grounds, because we have been told it by parents and teachers and other people whom we respect. What philosophical reasons are there for the belief?

It won't do to say that we ought to believe that science itself, or physics itself, can prove that science, or physics, provides the only ultimate explanations. We have to stand outside science and physics to make that judgement.

The main reasons given (for instance, by Smart) for adopting a purely physicalist view of the universe are as follows.

OCCAM'S RAZOR

The medieval philosopher William of Occam put forward the precept

'Do not multiply entities beyond necessity.'

In other words, if you can satisfactorily explain the universe by referring to n entities, do not try to explain it by referring to $n + 1$ entities. Thus if we can explain everything in the universe quite satisfactorily by referring to molecules and atoms and the still smaller particles of physics we ought not to try to introduce into our explanation any references to entities such as souls. Souls are superfluous.

Let us ask some questions about the precept itself. Occam's precept has primarily to do with explanation; it is only secondarily concerned with what exists. There might be things in the universe which are useless to us when we wish to explain things, but which exist nevertheless.

What is explanation? Is the best explanation the one which helps us to understand things and predict events? Or is it one which conforms to scientific theory? If we take the best explanation to be the one that fits best into (physical) scientific theory, we do not need Occam's Razor, or any other principle, to justify a physicalist–scientific world-view, for in that case our standard for the best explanation already presupposes that the physicalist–scientific world-view is correct. On the other hand, if we take the best explanation to be the one that helps us understand things and make predictions, then, while in astronomy, say, the best explanation will clearly turn out to be a scientific–mathematical one, when it comes to the behaviour of individual human beings ordinary commonsense folk psychology is usually better than any other explanatory model.

Occam's precept is adopted because it seems to work, because it helps rather than hinders the tasks of explanation and prediction. It is a methodological principle, and like any other methodological hypothesis it is tentative in its very nature: it might one day be supplanted by an anti-Occam precept for all we know!

PLAUSIBILITY

Smart and other physicalists appeal, sometimes implicitly and sometimes explicitly, to the supposed *plausibility* of the hypothesis that everything in the universe can be completely explained by reference to physics.

How powerful is an appeal to plausibility? It seems to me that there is no such thing as *initial* plausibility, and no objective standard of plausibility which exists prior to theory. Any claim that this or that proposition is plausible or implausible must presuppose theories before it can be regarded as objective. For example, any attempt to prove that the theory of reincarnation is objectively implausible must rely on some larger theoretical standpoint, probably some religious or scientific standpoint. Completely pre-theoretic assertions of plausibility must be completely subjective; what is plausible to me may seem very implausible to you. Furthermore the plausibility or implausibility of hypotheses and theories is culture-dependent in a high degree. Some nations think that the theory of recincarnation is quite plausible, others think it is utterly implausible.

Contingent Identity

The central thesis of physicalism (the identity theory) is that mental states and processes are nothing more than states of, or processes in, the brain. Mental states are *identical* with brain states.

Physicalists don't claim that the identity of mind and brain is an identity of meaning; they do not claim, for instance, that the word 'mind' means the same as the word 'brain', or that the word 'belief' means the same as 'such-and-such a neurological event'. The identity of mind and brain is contingent, not necessary: the world could have been otherwise, but it happens to be such that mental events happen to be brain events.

The notion of 'contingent identity' was introduced as part of a reply to objections made against materialist theories by philosophers of the school of linguistic analysis. These objectors argued that the logic of statements about brains and the logic of statements about minds are too different to allow identification of mental states with brain states. The main objections are as follows.

First of all, the known connections between mental events and brain events have been established by scientific research, that is, by experiment and empirical observation. Hence the connections themselves must be empirical and non-necessary. As such these connections are probably based on the relation of cause and effect.

The concepts of *thought*, *belief*, *desire*, *perception*, *sensation*, *emotion*, etc., predate by thousands of years the concepts of the science of physiology. To say that statements involving the former mean the same as statements involving the latter seems to imply that early man knew all about neuro-physiology, which is ridiculous.

Even today people can speak perfectly sensibly about their thoughts, beliefs, sensations and so on, without needing to know any facts about the physiology of the brain.

The notions of experience and consciousness are old and ordinary, whereas the technical terms of neuro-physiology are new, and their proper use is a matter of expertise. To say that the two sorts of notions mean the same is a bit like saying that 'bowled leg before wicket' means the same as some intricate proposition of anatomical mechanics.

The qualitative descriptions which apply to emotions and beliefs and sensations and so on – adjectives like *powerful*, *painful*, *agonising* – cannot be applied to brain processes; and conversely, the quantitative descriptions which apply to them – *rapid, short-term, located in the frontal lobe* and so on – cannot be applied to beliefs and emotions.

Finally, each individual has direct knowledge of his own states of mind: even the greatest neuro-physiologist in the world could know only indirectly, by inference, about another's state of mind. The greatest neuro-physiologist in the world can only see the events which 'normally go with' your headache, and your belief in God, and so on; he cannot experience these things directly unless he is you. What he sees (the brain events) therefore cannot be the same things as your beliefs and your pains.

In reply to objections of this kind Smart writes:

> The thesis that sensations are brain-processes . . . is not the thesis that e.g. 'after-image' or 'ache' mean the same as 'brain-process of sort X' . . . it is that, insofar as 'after-image' or 'ache' is a report of a process, etc., it is a report of a process that *happens to be* a brain-process. It follows that the thesis does not claim that sensation statements can be translated into statements about brain-processes. Nor does it claim that the logic of a sensation statement is the same as that of a brain-process statement.

Mental processes happen to be brain processes. They are identical with brain processes, but contingently, not necessarily.

Physicalism is prima facie vulnerable to objections based on a critique of the 'contingent identity thesis'. There are two possible criticisms that can be made of this thesis, one radical, the other less so. The less radical criticism is that the notion of contingent identity is ambiguous, covering a variety of different types of relation; and the more radical one is that there is no such thing as contingent identity at all.

Types of Identity Statement

Statements of identity are of various kinds.

MEANING IDENTITY

A statement of identity can be formed whenever two general nouns mean the same, that is, when they are synonyms; or, more generally, from any pair of synonyms, whether these be nouns or whole phrases.

Three examples (one language):

'Motor cars are [the same things as] automobiles.'
'Drooling is [the same thing as] dribbling.'
'Octagons are [the same things as] eight-angled plane figures.'

Two more, each involving two languages:

'Geschenke are [the same things as] presents.'
'An animal whose father is a yak and whose mother is a cow is [the same thing as] a dzong.'

Statements of meaning identity are found in dictionaries.

REFERENTIAL IDENTITY, *OR* NAME IDENTITY

A statement of identity can be formed whenever one person or object or event, or one precise group of persons or objects or events, has two different proper names. An example:

'Mt Everest is [the very same mountain as] Chomolungma.'

Generally speaking, statements of referential identity are not to be found in dictionaries.

CONTINGENT IDENTITY

Contingent identity is an important notion in twentieth-century philosophy mainly for the reasons explained above. But contingent identity statements, as it turns out, are not all of the same kind. They make up a ragbag collection of propositions, and there is disagreement about what belongs in the ragbag. Some philosophers include instances of name identity, for example, while others do not. We can say though that, like statements of meaning identity, contingent identity statements must be reversible. They must be such that whenever 'A is B' is true than 'B is A' is also true.
    Contingent identity may concern an individual.
    Here is an example:

'Mrs Thatcher is the first woman Prime Minister of Great Britain.'

This is reversible:

'The first woman PM . . . is Mrs Thatcher.'

In everyday speech statements of this type are used much like ordinary empirical descriptions, and can be combined with them without any sense of strangeness:

'Mrs Thatcher is Britain's first woman PM and my favourite politician.'

(Compare: 'Motor cars are automobiles and my favourite means of transport': this combines a meaning identity statement with an ordinary empirical description, and it sounds rather odd.)

Contingent identity may have to do with classes of things.

In some cases the identity of classes is contingent in the sense of being *accidental*. Suppose it were the case that the only berries eaten by Norwegians happened to be strawberries, and that no one else ever ate strawberries. The statement

'All berries eaten by Norwegians are strawberries and only Norwegians ever eat strawberries.'

identifies the class of berries eaten by Norwegians with the class of strawberries. However, the identity would be accidental and temporary and easily changed by innovative farmers and exporters.

Contrast the following:

'Hens are the only known animals with a normal body temperature of 109°F.'

This identity is presumably permanent, for there are probably reasons to be found in the theory of evolution which explain why it is in the nature of hens to have that body temperature rather than some other one. We have here a 'nature-statement', and it shows that contingent identity statements can be used to say things about how the world must be as well as about the way it just happens to be. However, the 'must' is not a logical 'must'.

Consider also this example:

'Hens are animals which have a body temperature of 109°F.'

This is an ordinary description from which we can create an identity statement simply by adding in the words 'the only animals which'. But the longer sentence tells us no more about hens than the shorter one; it merely adds some information about non-hens.

The relationship between being a hen and having a certain body temperature is not exactly accidental (probably), but there are other (putative) contingent identities which are, as it were, less accidental still. Here we might mention *constitutive identity*, of which the following are examples:

'Common salt is composed of sodium and chlorine in chemical combination.'

'Light is a stream of photons.'

It has sometimes been argued that the identity of mental events and brain events is, or is analogous to, constitutive identity. If this is right then mental events are in some sense *made up of* brain events.

I imagine that physicalists in general do not really believe that the alleged identity of mental events and brain events is a complete accident. They believe that the contingent identity of mind and brain must have something to do with natural laws.

Kripke's Objection

Saul Kripke has addressed himself to the question of contingent identity in his celebrated monograph *Naming and Necessity*. He argues that genuine identity must be necessary, otherwise it will not conform to Leibniz's Law. How could an object be *accidentally* identical with itself?

Kripke writes: 'many philosophers feel damned lucky that these examples [i.e. of supposed contingent identity] are around . . . [For they] hold to a thesis called "the identity thesis".'

The thesis of contingent identity, he says, is 'a dark doctrine'.

Kripke's monograph is written in an easy and expansive style. What follows is a précis and a gloss.

Kripke asserts:

1 Leibniz's Law of the Indiscernibility of Identicals is no less self-evident than the Law of Contradiction.

He then invents:

2 a new term, 'rigid designator', which he defines as 'a term which designates the same object in every possible world'.

One might perhaps quarrel with the definition, for instance on the grounds that it incorporates reference to a large semantic/ontological theory, the Possible Worlds Theory, which some hold to be absurd in one of its versions and contentious in all of them. Or one might hold that the philosophical accounts of Possible Worlds make no sense until one already has a coherent theory of identity (and maybe of rigid designation too), so that Kripke's definition of his own new term puts the cart before the horse. But to dispute the definition here would lead us too far away from the issue under discussion.

Kripke argues that:

3 Names of individuals, e.g. 'Cicero', and names of natural kinds and species, e.g. 'elephant', 'water', 'salt', 'gold', are rigid designators.

And he argues that:

4 Identity statements constructed with two rigid designators are *necessary truths*; but identity statements constructed otherwise are not in all cases necessary truths.

He also argues that:

5 How one knows that a statement is true is separate from the question as to whether it is a necessary truth. Thus it is possible to discover a necessary truth by empirical means.

And he argues that:

6 The identity of an object with itself can be expressed either by statements which are necessary, or by statements which are not. Hence the non-necessity of a *statement* of identity does not mean that the *thing* referred to in it is non-necessarily identical with itself. The very idea that a thing could be non-necessarily identical with itself is a nonsense.

Kripke considers, and to my mind succeeds in refuting, some arguments which purport to show that there can be such a relation as contingent identity. His refutations rest on the propositions which I have labelled 4, 5 and 6.

The physicalistic argument that

SINCE one can use the name 'Cicero' to refer to Cicero and the name 'Tully' to refer to Cicero also, and not know that Cicero is

Tully, IT FOLLOWS that the statement 'Cicero is Tully' is contingent
if true.

is not a valid argument.

It is not valid because its premise implies only that the truth of
an identity statement need not be known a priori but can also be
known a posteriori.

Its premise does not imply that statements not known a priori
must be contingent.

Some identity statements about the various natural kinds and
species (such as gold, or water, or elephants) are expressions of
scientific laws. They say something about the *nature* or about the
basic constituents of gold, or elephants, or whatever. Such statements
can take one of two possible forms.

First, it may be that one rigid designator (e.g. 'common salt') is
linked with another (e.g. 'NaCl'). These statements, if true, are
therefore not contingent but necessary: see 4 above.

Second, it may be that a rigid designator and a non-rigid
designator are linked. In that case, the statement need not be a
necessary statement even if it is true. But that in no way shows
that the natural kind referred to is only 'contingently identical' with
itself: see 6 above.

Kripke's theses about the nature of identity have important
consequences for physicalism. If minds and mental processes, and
brains and brain processes, are natural kinds, then 'mental processes'
and 'brain processes' are rigid designators. Therefore the putative
identity statement 'mental processes are [just the same things as]
brain processes' is, if true, a necessary truth not a contingent truth.
So if the statement 'mental processes are brain processes' is true,
then the identity of mental processes and brain processes (the
'things') is (of course) necessary *and also* the identity statement
itself is a necessary truth. Hence the identity is not contingent at
either level.

The problem for physicalism now is that physicalists themselves
accepted the early arguments against the proposition that there is
any *necessary* connection between mental events and brain events.

(Still, it should be noted that some of those early anti-physicalist
arguments turn out to be invalid if we accept Kripke's account of
identity. Thus the fact that the identity of mind and brain would
have to be discovered empirically is of course easily explained by
his thesis that necessary truths can be discovered empirically.)

To sum up Kripke's objections:

The very idea of the 'contingent identity' of things is inconsistent with Leibniz's Law.

The contingent identity thesis rests on false suppositions about necessary truths and how they are learnt.

Finally, he argues as follows:

If mental states are identified with causal roles, which in turn are identified with the causal roles of brain states,

then, since the fact that a certain brain state has a certain causal role must be contingent,

it follows that the fact that a particular mental state *is* that particular mental state, i.e. *is itself*, must also be contingent,

and that would be tantamount to saying of particular mental states that they are not always those particular mental states, which is self-evidently absurd.

Kripke concludes:

> the correspondence between a brain state and a mental state seems to have a certain element of contingency. We have seen that identity is not a relation which can hold contingently between objects. Therefore, if the identity thesis were correct, the element of contingency would not lie in the relation between the mental and the physical states. It cannot lie . . . in the relation between the phenomenon . . . and the way it is felt or appears . . . since in the case of mental phenomena there is no 'appearance' beyond the mental phenomenon itself . . . Materialism must hold . . . that any mental facts are 'ontologically dependent' on physical facts in the straight-forward sense of following from them by *necessity*. (my italics)

But, he adds, intuition tells us that there is no such necessity.

3

Functionalism

The Turing Machine

The mathematician Alan Turing made important theoretical and practical contributions to the early development of computers. One of his most significant ideas was the notion of an idealised computer, which he called a Universal Computer, and which is also sometimes called a Turing Machine. In 1936 Turing, using his notion of the Universal Computer, was able to show that a method capable of deciding the truth or falsity of any mathematical assertion whatsoever is an impossibility; mathematics must therefore contain unsolvable problems.

Turing wrote a paper about artificial intelligence which was published in *Mind* in 1950. In it he said:

> I believe that in about 50 years' time . . . the use of words and general educated opinion will have altered so much that one will be able to speak of machines thinking without expecting to be contradicted.

He defended his prediction by describing a thought experiment which he called 'the imitation game'. This imaginary game, he suggested, shows that the abilities of digital computers are in principle indistinguishable from human intellectual capacities.

In the game a Turing machine or ideal computer is placed in a room and attached to a teleprinter which is outside the room. A man is also in the room, and can send out messages via the same teleprinter. Questions are sent into the room by a human questioner and answered sometimes by the computer and sometimes by the man. In the game the machine dodges questions it cannot answer; so too, presumably, does the man.

Without the clues offered by sound of voice, appearance, etc., the questioner, according to Turing, would have only a 70 per cent chance of being able to distinguish the man from the machine on the basis of the answers given to five minutes' questioning.

I do not know why Turing said 70 per cent, and chose five minutes; nor do I see why he thought these figures indicate that the machine's 'intellectual' behaviour is indistinguishable from the man's. The argument does not seem very convincing, and indeed John Searle has used a somewhat similar thought experiment (the 'Chinese Room') as a way of trying to show that machines *don't* think – see below.

Turing is a parent of the philosophical doctrine of functionalism. David Lewis claims that D. M. Armstrong and he himself are the real parents, but maybe a theory can have three or more parents.

In his 1950 paper Turing mentions Charles Babbage, a nineteenth-century mathematician who designed a mechanical computer which however was never completely built. Turing remarks:

> The fact that Babbage's Analytical Engine was to be entirely mechanical will help us to rid ourselves of a superstition. Importance is often attached to the fact that modern digital computers are electrical, and that the nervous system also is electrical. Since Babbage's machine was not electrical, and since all digital computers are in a sense equivalent, we see that this use of electricity cannot be of theoretical importance. . . . In the nervous system chemical phenomena are at least as important as electrical. In certain computers the storage system is mainly acoustic. . . . If we wish to find . . . similarities we should look rather for *mathematical analogies of function*. (my italics)

Functionalism and Physicalism

The theory of functionalism is sometimes expressed in the language of computing machines and artificial intelligence, and sometimes as if it were just a sophisticated version of physicalism.

The movement of ideas from physicalism to functionalism can be illustrated by reference to two papers published in 1965 and 1978 respectively – 'The Nature of Mind' by D. M. Armstrong and 'Mad pain and Martian pain' by David Lewis.

In his 1965 paper Armstrong states that the only kind of enquiry which produces consensus is scientific enquiry. From that it follows, he says, that the only good reasons we can have for our theoretical beliefs, including our beliefs about the nature of mankind, are the 'verdicts' given us by modern science. Hence he holds that the only really good reason we can have for holding a theoretical belief is the fact that everyone else, or nearly everyone else, has the same belief. He seems to overlook the historical fact that science has not been the only body of belief backed up by consensus. It is probably not the most powerful consensus even today.

Modern science, says Armstrong 'can give a complete account of man *in purely physico-chemical terms*'. He adds: 'those scientists who still reject the physico-chemical account of man do so primarily for philosophical or religious reasons, and only secondarily, and half-heartedly, for reasons of scientific detail.'

Armstrong sets up consensus as a test for truth, even though the fact of consensus is not itself a premise or part of physical or chemical science. To set up consensus as a test for truth is a philosophical enterprise, not a scientific one; it is on a par with the reasons held by the anti-materialist scientists whose standpoint Armstrong condemns. His rejection of the philosophical or other exterior-to-science reasoning of scientists is a mistake, because if the exterior-to-science reasonings of scientists are valueless merely on account of the fact that they are exterior then Armstrong's own arguments must also be valueless for the same reason. Armstrong is defending science, not doing it; he is a handmaiden, not a practitioner; his own reasoning is exterior to science.

It seems better to adopt the principle that reasoning, whether scientific or not, must stand or fall on its own merits,

The premise that mental states are the cause of behaviour does not by itself entail the truth of physicalism, but, says Armstrong, it makes physicalism possible; for 'It [then] becomes a scientific question what in fact the intrinsic nature of that cause might be . . . [it] might be a spiritual substance . . . it might be breath . . . it might be many other things.' And he goes on: 'in fact the verdict of modern science seems to be that the sole cause of mind-betokening behaviour in man and the higher animals is the physico-chemical workings of the central nervous system . . . assuming we have correctly characterised our concept of a mental state as nothing but the cause of behaviour, then we can identify these mental states with purely physical states of the central nervous system.'

David Lewis and Martian Pain

The characterisation of mental states as causes, and the presupposition that these causes are intrinsically physico-chemical, does not of course necessitate the conclusion that mental states are *brain* states. David Lewis notes this when he describes how a functionalist account allows for there to be 'Martian pain'.

Lewis constructs a thought-experiment about Martians as follows. Imagine that Martians exist and that they behave like human beings. Must we suppose that their mental states are brain states? Not at all: they might not have brains like ours; they might not have brains at all. It might be that they have hydraulic feet and that the occurrence of Martian pain goes with an increase in hydraulic pressure in Martian feet, rather than with anything happening in their heads.

Let us suppose then, that in Martians the functional role of causing pain-behaviour is filled or held by the happenings in Martian feet. As a functionalist Lewis identifies Martian pain with the function, or causal role, of producing pain-behaviour in Martians. If the facts were as described in the thought-experiment it would be the happenings in Martian feet which filled the causal role; it follows, Lewis concludes, that those hydraulic foot-happenings would therefore be the very same thing as Martin pain.

Many functionalists hold that human pain can probably be identified as specific states of the brain – the human brain, of course! But they allow, what after all is obvious, that pain in other animals cannot be a state of a human brain. Indeed in some non-human animals (or in Martians) pain might be constituted by states of organs other than the brain, for example, the states of the Martians' hydraulic feet. For this reason Lewis says 'the concept pain is non-rigid and the word "pain" is a non-rigid designator'. In other words, it is a contingent matter what kind of state the concept and the word apply to – contingent, *inter alia*, on what kind of creature we are talking about.

Is Lewis right about the contingency of the connection between pain and the word 'pain'?

Lewis's functional analysis of pain has three terms and involves two assertions of identity, so it can be represented schematically as:

$$A = B = C.$$

Let us use the symbol RCR to mean The Right Causal Role. Then Lewis's functionalism can be expressed as a double equivalence:

Pain = RCR = performance by hydraulic feet OR by brain fibres OR . . .

The double equivalence has to do both with meanings and with contingencies. The first equation sign represents a meaning-identity and the second one represents a contingency. Pain is *necessarily* the cause of pain-behaviour; and brain events (or feet events or whatever) are *contingently* identical with that cause in various different real or logically possible creatures.

Three questions suggest themselves here.

First, is the notion of a function clear and unambiguous? Is Lewis's conception of a function the same as Turing's, for example?

Next, does a functionalist account provide conditions of mentality which are both necessary and sufficient? Can such an account stand the test of counter-examples?

Third, if pain, and other mental events, can be properly understood only as roles, then the names of mental events and processes would indeed be non-rigid designators, as Lewis affirms. But is this a plausible view of mental events?

What Is a Function?

The etymological meaning of the verb *to function* is *to perform*.

The chief meanings of the noun *function* are as follows.

A function is a special kind of activity proper to a thing; its mode of action whereby it fulfils its purpose. The 'thing' may be a physical object or a physical organ ('the function of the eye is to see'; 'the function of a kettle is to boil water'), or an intellectual power ('the function of conscience is to warn'), or even a system or other abstraction. The State for example has a function, and its operational sub-systems also have functions. In this sense the word means roughly the same as the word 'purpose'.

Somewhat analogously the function of a person is constituted by types of action which are proper to that individual, but not, as it were, proper to him or her *qua* person. Rather, the function of a person is the activity proper to him or her *qua* member of some group or profession or *qua* holder of some office. By extension we may speak of the function of the office itself; and more generally, of the function (or purpose) of a profession or employment or trade. Thus we can speak about the functions ('official duties') of some individual, and about the functions of the Chief Electrician, and about the functions of electricians.

The *Oxford English Dictionary* does not give any examples of states or processes having functions. However, functionalism attributes functions precisely to states, processes and happenings. Now, does it make sense to speak of the functions of states, processes and happenings? For if not, then this theory is only a nonsense. However I think it does make sense. For instance, an individual cat's state of pregnancy has a function or purpose from the point of view of the survival of her species. Also it seems obvious that tasks have purposes or functions, and surely the carrying out of a task must be a process or a happening.

In mathematics a function is 'a variable quantity regarded in its relation to one or more other variables in terms of which it may be expressed, or on the value of which its own value depends'. This sense of the word is due to Leibniz, who in a paper of 1692 defined functions as the 'offices' which a straight line may fulfil in relation to a curve, viz., its tangent, normal, etc.

The mathematical idea of a function can be approached via the idea of variables.

One sort of 'variable' is simply a temporarily unknown quantity whose value is determined by constants, not by other variables. (In such case it seems to me that the idea of function applies in a somewhat degenerate sense.)

Example: x in the equation

$$x = \text{the atomic number of gold multiplied by } \pi.$$

Another kind of variable is the sort whose values are determined by the values of another variable.

Example: the variable x in the formula

$$x = 2\pi r.$$

Here the values of the variable x are determined by those of another variable (r) and it is proper to speak of x as a function of r.

Which sense of 'function' have functionalists in mind as the key concept of their theory? Is 'function' to be taken as analogous to mathematical functions, or not?

The Lewisite kind of function is not analogous to a mathematical function, it is a *role*, and a role which is filled by quite specialised performances or happenings. Lewisite functionalists speak of mental states or processes as roles filled by happenings temporally located between 'inputs' (for example, perceptions) and 'outputs' (for example, physical actions). Lewisite or role functionalists take it that the values of the 'variable' which they are concerned with have to be happenings; there is an underlying presumption that only happenings can be causes. This is a more than purely formal presupposition.

In brief:

There are some philosophical functionalists who, following Turing, think of the functions of functionalism as analogous to mathematical functions. To them 'is a function' means something like 'is determined by . . .'.

But there are other philosophical functionalists who, following David Lewis, think of functions as roles. To them 'is a function' means roughly 'performs such and such a job'.

I think it is far from clear that the two uses of the word 'function', that is, the non-mathematical use and the mathematical analogue, are interchangeable. The quasi-mathematical sense is system-dependent in a way in which the more ordinary idea of a function as a role is not. Or perhaps one might say that the mathematical analogue gets it sense from a formal system whereas the role notion belongs to an informal system (the system of ordinary language). It might be that there are really two kinds of functionalism therefore. Perhaps one day the functionalists will sort this question out for us.

Objections to Functionalism: Block's Conglomerate 'Mind'

Ned Block argues that, as an account of mind or mental states and processes, functionalism is too wide, in that it includes arrangements of matter which no one would describe as mental. In support of this thesis he has invented a thought-experiment which is supposed to prove that functionalism will classify as minds logically possible entities which we know are not minds.

He begins with the functionalist proposition that minds have inputs (e.g. perception) and outputs (i.e. behaviour). He then imagines what he calls a 'scenario' in which all the members of a nation of 1,000 million people (China perhaps) are issued with two-way radios that connect them to each other and also to radio satellites which give 'instructions' to an artificial body, some sort of robot. The system of 1,000 million people communicating with one another and with satellites plays the role of an external 'brain' connected to the artificial body by radio. Thus the arrangement mimics the relationship between the millions of brain cells in a human head, and their means of 'communication' with one another (whatever those are), and the effects which the intercommunications have on the human body, in so far as these effects are human actions.

(It is only fair to say that Block's own description of his thought-experiment is far more detailed than the above.)

Block argues that such a conglomeration is logically possible, but he thinks that, although it fulfils functionalist criteria for mentality, the system of 1,000 million people plus satellites would not be a mind, and the workings of the envisaged system would not constitute mental states and processes. Such an arrangement could perhaps be said to mimic, or simulate, mentality in some of its aspects but it is not an example of mentality.

It is not an example of mentality partly because of its size. Nations occupy large areas of space. It is counter-intuitive to suppose that minds could be spatially huge conglomerates. If minds could be spatially huge conglomerates then the intercontinental ballistic nuclear missile systems might be minds. Some people perhaps even think so. But it is hard to see how such an idea can escape the charge of idolatry.

What else are our (counter-) intuitions based on? Well, the arrangement described in Block's thought-experiment has no subjective experiences apart from the individual subjective experiences of the 1,000 million individuals. But these are irrelevant; if the system were a mind, it – the system as such – would have a set of subjective experiences of its own. For in the thought-experiment it is the whole system which supposedly exemplifies a (functionalist) mind.

In other words, the functionalist definition of mentality is too wide, it lets in too much, it would force us against the grain to accept Block's conglomerate as a mind, not to mention other possible arrangements that might be produced as thought-experiments by other ingenious thought-experimenters.

Objections to Functionalism: Searle's Chinese Room

One kind of funtionalism sees mental states as being somewhat similar to computer programs. Computer programs are independent of their realisations. One and the same program can be realised in different ways.

John Searle has invented a thought-experiment designed to test the philosophical theory that the instantiation of a sufficiently complex computer program would be an instance of the mental state or process of *understanding*. We will call this *the Chinese Room thought-experiment*. It is a variation on Turing's Imitation Game.

Suppose that you are an English-speaking monoglot locked in a soundproof room with a two-way video communication system linking you to people outside the room. Inside the room you find two separate batches of what is in fact Chinese writing. But you have no knowledge at all of the Chinese language either written or spoken and cannot tell Chinese script from Cyrillic or any other exotic script. In other words, you do not know that the squiggles on the batches of paper are symbols in a written language.

The people outside the room have names for these batches: they call the first batch 'a script' and the second batch 'a story': but they do not tell you this.

Also inside the room there is a book containing a set of rules, written in English, which correlates the first batch of squiggles with the second batch. These rules enable you to correlate two sets of symbols which you can identify only by their shapes.

Next you find in the room a third batch of squiggles. The people outside the room call this batch 'questions' but they do not tell you that.

Then you find a second rule book, in the English language. The rules in this book enable you to correlate elements in the third batch ('questions') with those in the other two batches ('script' and 'story'). Again you make your correlations purely by examining the shapes of the symbols.

Finally you find some instructions, in English, which tell you how to give out on your video equipment certain symbols with certain shapes to people outside the room in response to their giving you various shapes from the third batch ('questions').

The people outside the room who are feeding shapes to you call the shapes you send out to them 'answers' but they do not tell you that.

They also call the first two sets of rules in English 'the program' but they do not tell you that.

After a while you get so good at symbol manipulation that anyone outside who did not know about you would believe that you were a native Chinese speaker.

Searle says that you would be behaving like a computer, producing answers, which you don't know are answers, by manipulating symbols, which you do not know are symbols but can recognise by their shapes. As far as the Chinese script, stories, questions and answers are concerned, you are an instantiation of a computer program. But you don't know you are such an instantiation.

It is pretty obvious that the person in the Chinese Room does not understand the stories or the questions or the answers. To see this all you need to do is to imagine that you are the person in the Chinese Room. Or suppose that a native Chinese speaker is also working in the Room, without, however, communicating in any way with the other occupant. The inputs and outputs of the Chinese speaker will be indistinguishable from the inputs and outputs of the non-Chinese speaker. Yet it seems clear that the Chinese speaker understands the stories and the questions and the answers whereas the other person does not.

If Searle is correct then instantiation of the right kind of program is not a sufficient condition for the presence of the mental state of understanding.

Objections to Functionalism: Is Pain Only a Role?

Expressions of the form 'cause of such-and-such' designate non-rigidly, assuming we accept a Humean or quasi-Humean account of causation.

Now, can expressions like 'cause of . . .' ever by themselves capture the intrinsic natures of real items in the real world? There seems something wrong with this idea. Can the intrinsic nature of Bill Sykes be captured entirely via a collection of predicates like 'whoever caused the disappearance of the family silver'?

At certain stages of scientific enquiry, as the physicalists have rightly said, though not perhaps in these words, some entities, such as genes and neutrinos, are theoretical entities only. As such they will be picked out by non-rigid designators. At certain stages of scientific enquiry the meaning of a word such as 'gene' can be explained only via the concepts of cause, effect and behaviour pattern. When that is the case then in other possible worlds the entity which explained the facts about the inheritance of natural characteristics need not be made up of chromosomes, nor be part of a molecule shaped like a helix.

To my mind, ordinary familiar items and stuffs (such as mountains, individual people, salt, gold and so on) are not theoretical entities. They can be and usually are given labels or descriptions which designate rigidly.

Classificatory science often produces new designators, subdividing classes of things that seemed originally to be more similar than they actually are. However new names, for instance new technical terms, do not necessarily have to replace old ones, nor do old terms necessarily lose rigidity when new ones are introduced. 'Common salt' and 'NaCl' and 'mercury' and 'Hg' are all rigid designators. Mendeleef's table lists the elements according to certain classificatory principles and labels them with names, some of which are old, like 'gold', and some of which are fairly new, like 'plutonium'. These labels are clearly intended to designate rigidly.

One result of scientific investigation is to enable us to give rigid designators to previously unlocated items by locating them. For instance, suppose someone sets out to find the cause of AIDS. When he begins his research he has to use the phrase 'the cause of AIDS', which is a non-rigid designator describing a role or slot in the world filled by an unknown item. Suppose that our investigator discovers that the item which fits this role or slot (in our world) is in fact a virus which has certain characteristics that enable people with the right laboratory equipment to re-identify it. This virus he labels 'HIV'. The label 'HIV' is a rigid designator; for although 'the cause of AIDS' may refer to different items in different possible worlds, 'HIV' refers to a type of virus, that is, to physical entities which are located in space and which have a typical shape and other typical properties in all possible worlds. It is that kind of label. This can be seen from the fact that it is logically possible that HIV could turn out to be only one of several causes of AIDS and logically possible that HIV could turn out to be completely unconnected with the disease.

If functionalism is correct the word 'pain' is not analogous to the word 'HIV' it is not a rigid designator. It only means and can only mean 'whatever causes such-and-such behaviour'. 'Pain' refers to nothing more than a role, a role which is filled by various role-fillers which produce pain-behaviour in various different sorts of creature. If functionalism is correct there is an indefinitely large set of possible role-fillers each one of which is capable of producing pain-behaviour in at least one possible world. If functionalism is correct pain itself is at one level only a role and at another level only a large disjunction of possible states of affairs in human and other brains and Martian feet and so on. Roles and disjunctions are at best merely theoretical entities; so on this account pain is only a (rather dubious) theoretical entity.

Yet surely pain must be something more than a theoretical entity! Pain is extremely familiar and ordinary, it belongs to the world of facts, not the world of theory, virtually every human being experiences it, and it is only commonsense to suppose that all the members of all the higher animal species are familiar with pain. How could such an item be intrinsically theoretical?

Pains and many other mental states and processes are directly experienced by the subject. The criteria of similarity and difference in the case of many mental states, including pain, are phenomenological, which is to say, the criteria consist in how the states in question feel or seem to the subject. When a migraine sufferer says that s/he has 'the same kind of headache as usual' or 'a typical migraine headache' or 'not a migraine headache this time, thank goodness' everyone understands the language used and every normal person knows that the similarity or dissimilarity is phenomenological. No one thinks of the similarity or dissimilarity as being in any important way a matter of the causal role of headaches. Still less is it the case that such similarities and dissimilarities are relationships which can be identified only through the causal roles of various kinds of pain.

More About the Turing Machine

Turing predicted that 50 years after he wrote people would accept that computers have intellectual abilities not unlike those of human beings, and would speak, quite naturally, of computers thinking 'without expecting to be contradicted'.

In the 38 years that have passed since he made that claim the use of computers has become extremely widespread, the varieties available are legion, and the capacities of the machines themselves possibly exceed anything he ever imagined. Yet it seems to me that Turing's prophecy has not been fulfilled. Everyone knows that computers can *compute*, of course; but the idea that they can think is not widely accepted, and for every philosopher or computer scientist who claims that these machines are thinking there will be a dozen to contradict that proposition.

Computers simulate various human mental processes of a mathematical and logical nature. What does this simulation prove?

Let us consider some different senses of the word 'simulate'.[1]

1 'Simulate' can mean 'represent', or 'model'. It is in this sense of the word that war games simulate war. In the example a theory

[1] I have taken the examples which illustrate different kinds of simulation from a lecture given by Hugh Mellor in Cambridge in 1986. I am grateful to Professor Mellor for allowing me to borrow his thoughts.

about war is embodied in the choice of the data which make up the game or model of war. These pieces of data are the premises used to predict possible outcomes of certain strategies in war.

If a computer could simulate mental processes in this sense that would not prove that the computer is actually performing mental processes, that it is actually thinking, that it is a mind. No one thinks that a war game is a real war.

2 'Simulate' can mean 'represent dynamically and pictorially'. In this sense of the word a planetarium simulates the galaxy and an action replay film of an incident in a football match simulates the incident in the football match. But no one thinks the planetarium *is* a galaxy, no one thinks the action replay *is* an incident in a football match. If a computer could simulate mental processes in this sense of the word that would not prove that the computer is a mind.

3 'Simulate' can mean simply 'is easily mistaken for'. In this sense of the word a *trompe l'oeil* painting simulates its subject. We can also say that a very good planetarium just might be mistaken for the galaxy in certain circumstances of observation.

From the point of view of the people outside Searle's Chinese Room the non-speaker of Chinese inside the Room simulates a Chinese speaker in this sense of the word. The Turing machine too simulates thought in this rather minimal sense. In the Imitation Game a computer can be mistaken for a man. But if an entity can be mistaken for a thinking thing, that does not prove that it *is* a thinking thing. No one holds the philosophical view that *trompe l'oeil* paintings *are* the cups and saucers etc. which they depict.

4 'Simulate' can mean 'does the same job as . . .' An aeroplane does the same job as a ship, it carries people to, say, the Bahamas. Computers can do some of the same jobs as human beings do – arithmetic is an obvious example – but that does not prove that the computers are thinking. The fact that computers perform some tasks far more rapidly than human beings also does not prove that they are thinking. The fact that you can get to the Bahamas faster in an aeroplane than in a ship does not prove that the aeroplane floats on the sea any more than it proves that the ship flies through the air. Human beings do arithmetic by thinking; it is virtually certain that computers do arithmetic some other way.

Some important though not very large items would need to be removed from a planetarium before it could be a galaxy; for instance, the labels saying 'Built by Ptolemy and Co., Suppliers of

Planetaria to the Gentry' would have to be removed. But a great deal more would need to be *added* to a planetarium before it could be a galaxy.

The computer's enormous speed in making mathematical calculations makes it unlike any human calculator, so maybe that would need to be removed before a computer could be much like a human mind. Perhaps too the invisible labels which read 'Made by Human Beings for Human Use' would have to be removed. But a great deal more, perhaps galactically more, would need to be added to a computer than taken away from it before it could be a mind.

We might compare the question, Are minds merely computers? with the similar question, Are mental processes physical energy transfers? Suppose for the sake of argument we agree that mental processes are simply physical energy transfers – the doctrine of physicalism. We still need to know just *what kinds* of physical energy transfers mental processes are; we need to distinguish *mental* physical energy transfers from the thousands of other kinds of physical energy transfers – for instance, the physical energy transfers that take place in galaxies, and in refrigerators, and in bakers' ovens, and in batteries, and in internal combustion engines, etc.

Finally let us consider the slogan, 'Mind is to brain as software is to hardware.' A serious objection to this slogan is that there is an evident lack of analogy in regard to production. We know that the computer hardware does not produce (initiate) the program. But it is highly probable that the brain helps produce the mental state.

Part II
Linguistic Analysis

4

Language and Forms of Life: Wittgenstein

The Absence of Theories

Wittgenstein's posthumously published books and notebooks are overwhelmingly concerned with three large philosophical topics: language and meaning, mind, and mathematics. His major work, the *Philosophical Investigations*, is mainly concerned with the first two, and there is more material in it on philosophy of mind than on meaning and language.

Part I of the *Investigations* consists of 172 pages divided into 693 paragraphs or 'remarks', of which paragraphs 1–136 are concerned with language and paragraphs 172–239 with the concept of following a rule; and the rest of Part I is about thought, perception, sensation, emotion and understanding. Part II is made up of 60 pages divided into 14 sections, all quite short except for section xi, which is 36 pages long. Of the 14 sections, 11 (including section xi) are about such things as fear, hope, sense-impressions, dreaming, grief, seeing-as, mental images, belief, the soul, thoughts, knowledge, motives, memory and the present character of psychology as a science.

Yet for all that, as it seems to me, Wittgenstein has no theory of the mind except in so far as he has a theory about philosophy in general. In fact, neither in the *Philosophical Investigations* nor in any of his other later writings are any theories at all to be found apart from a theory about the nature of philosophy. This theory about philosophy in general is mainly to be seen in the answers Wittgenstein gives to three connected questions, viz.: What gives rise to philosophical problems? How can philosophical problems be solved? and What methods of enquiry are unsuited to philosophy?

What Philosophy Is Not

Many English-speaking professional philosophers, as we have seen, are nowadays inclined to believe that philosophy should develop theories which reflect and in some sense incorporate the discoveries of the natural sciences. They tend to think of philosophy as a handmaiden to science, or at any rate as a discipline which *ought* to be a handmaiden to science. (In practice this scientistic project is applied to only one branch of philosophy, namely, philosophy of mind or philosophical psychology.)

A somewhat older but still current idea is that philosophy itself is a kind of primitive science, made up of a conglomerate of unrelated and relatively unsuccessful enquiries which as time passes split off from philosophy and become true successful sciences with clear boundaries between their subject matters.

Wittgenstein's writings about the nature of philosophy and the nature of empirical science involve a rejection of both these ideas about what philosophy is or ought to be; he holds that the methods of science and the methods of philosophy are radically different. This can be seen from his notebooks and letters as well as in the *Blue and Brown Books* and the *Philosophical Investigations*.

In the *Blue and Brown Books* Wittgenstein writes: 'Philosophers constantly see the method of science before their eyes, and are irresistibly tempted to ask and answer questions in the way science does. This tendency is the real source of metaphysics, and leads the philosopher into complete darkness.' He is using the word 'metaphysics' here as the logical positivists used it, i.e. pejoratively.

The method of science is the method of reducing the explanation of natural phenomena to the smallest possible number of primitive natural laws. Philosophers attempt to imitate the method of science because of a 'craving for generality', but looking for general explanations is not appropriate to philosophical enquiry. Wittgenstein writes: 'I want to say here that it can never be our job to reduce anything to anything.'

Earlier, in a note made in 1930, and published after his death in the collection of notes called (in English) *Culture and Value*, he says:

Our civilisation is characterised by the word 'progress'. Progress is its form rather than making progress being one of its features. Typically it constructs. It is occupied with building an ever more

complicated structure [he means an intellectual structure, a generalised theory]. And even clarity is sought only as a means to this end,
not as an end in itself. For me on the contrary clarity, perspicuity
are valuable in themselves.

It is perhaps worth noting that Wittgenstein also questioned two
assumptions that are commonly made about science, namely, that its
results are always beneficial, and that its practitioners typically have
intellectually open and enquiring attitudes. For example, he wrote in
1930: 'Man has to awaken to wonder – and so perhaps do peoples.
Science is a way of sending him to sleep again.' And in a letter
written to Norman Malcolm in December 1945 he said: 'extraordinary
scientific achievements have a way these days of being used for the
destruction of human beings (I mean their bodies, or their souls, *or
their intelligence*). *So hold onto your brains.*'
In 1947 he wrote:

> It isn't absurd to believe . . . that the age of science and technology
> is the beginning of the end for humanity; that the idea of great
> progress is a delusion, along with the idea that the truth will ultimately
> be known; that there is nothing good or desirable about scientific
> knowledge and that mankind, in seeking it, is falling into a trap. It
> is by no means obvious that this is not how things are.

Language and Philosophy

Wittgenstein says in the Preface of the *Philosophical Investigations*
that the book is 'really only an album'. Indeed all his later works
consist of notebooks or 'albums' made up of more or less aphoristic
remarks. In this he resembles Nietzsche.

Also in the Preface he says that his original intention was to weld
his thoughts into a consecutive series of ideas. But he found this
impossible to do: 'my thoughts were soon crippled if I tried to force
them on in any direction against their natural inclination. – And
this was, of course, connected with the very nature of the
investigation. For this compels us to travel over a wide field of
thought criss-cross in every direction.'

The need for criss-cross travel comes from the nature of the
enquiry.

What is its nature, then?

There are four linked elements which deserve mention. One
thing which Wittgenstein often says is that language creates

philosophical problems. ('Philosophy is a battle against the bewitchment of our intelligence by means of language.') Some commentators, including Gellner (see below), take this dictum as embodying the whole of Wittgenstein's later philosophy. But in fact Wittgenstein's later books do not appear to be based on the dictum that language as such is the only cause of philosophical problems. Rather, it seems, it is the interplay between language and life which we don't understand. Philosophical understanding must include an understanding of 'forms' or 'patterns' of life. This in turn is linked with the suggestion, implied rather than stated, that it is not language, but a feature or tendency innate in humanity which causes philosophical 'bewitchment'. This innate tendency expresses itself in an overpowering desire to simplify and to generalise. Finally, it appears from Wittgenstein's actual practice that he held that philosophical enquiry if it is to be illuminating must include detailed investigations into the connections between (and differences between) the concepts of 'ordinary' thought.

In the early sections of the *Philosophical Investigations* he often mentions the great multiplicity of the types of words and sentences which go to make up a natural language, and he says that human beings are prone to assimilate all those different types to one model. We human beings tend to think that language consists of words each of which is correlated with something in the world outside language. We further suppose that the correlated objects give words their meanings. So the red things in the world give meaning to the word 'red', for instance. But this view of language is radically mistaken. Words and sentences are like tools in a tool box, they have different uses; and we are like ignoramuses who think that every tool in the tool box is a hammer.

Maybe the appeal of a simplified theory of language is due to the fact that words, unlike tools, actually all look much the same. Tools look different from one another, they look *essentially* different; whereas words do not look essentially different from one another, their phonetic and scriptive differences are arbitrary. The arbitrariness of the differences between words, regarded as sounds or marks on paper, is shown by the fact that different sounds can have the same meaning and the same sound can have different meanings.

Words and sentences are to be distinguished from each other by their uses. If we look carefully at the way words are used in real life we will see a huge manifold of subtle differences and similarities which is ignored by generalisers and philosophical theorisers.

The theory that the objects and events in the world give meaning to language is less misleading for some words and sentences than for others. This simplified view of language is surely less misleading for words like 'cat' and sentences like 'the cat is on the mat' than it is for words like 'and', 'or' and 'but' and phrases like 'in spite of' and 'for the sake of'. Nevertheless the idea that objects and states of affairs give words their meanings is essentially misleading for all words. This Wittgensteinian thesis is particularly important for his view of the mind. He often says that events in the head cannot give meaning to words like 'understand', 'hope', 'believe' and so on.

Another mistake which humanity constantly makes is to suppose that, when things fall under general notions, and are referred to with so-called 'common nouns', this must be because the things in question share one or more common features. But that does not have to be the case at all. Wittgenstein illustrates this point with the example of the common noun 'game'. Games do not all share a common feature, instead there are many overlapping features, rather like family resemblances and rather like fibres in a rope; so that some games share some features with some other games though no game shares any one feature with all the others. He writes:

> don't think, but look! – Look for example at board games, with their multifarious relationships. Now pass to card games; here you find many correspondences with the first group, but many common features drop out, and others appear. When we pass to ball-games, much that is common is retained, but much is lost. – Are they all 'amusing'? Compare chess with noughts and crosses. Or is there always winning and losing, or competition between players? Think of patience. . . .

Now this idea that the items which fall under one concept might well have no one feature or set of features common to all of them is also very important for Wittgenstein's work in the philosophy of mind. He repeatedly says that psychological concepts are of this kind.

Psychological Concepts and 'Family Resemblances'

In the *Investigations* and other later writings the notion that a concept can be as it were made up of overlapping 'fibres' or 'family resemblances' is repeatedly mentioned in connection with psychology. Different instances of understanding, for instance, are said to be like different games, having no one element in common but rather a series of overlapping features each of which is common to some cases of understanding but not to all. And the same is true of memory, belief, fear and perception.

If Wittgenstein had said that *all* concepts are 'family resemblance' concepts that would amount to a general theory about concepts. However I think that at this point we must follow the recommendation 'don't think – but look!'

To begin with let us look at the texts. Wittgenstein nowhere says explicitly that all concepts are family resemblance concepts. The only ones he discusses explicitly are games, numbers and the psychological concepts. He also mentions colours in this context.

Next let us look at concepts. Aren't they in fact very different one from the other?

The reason why two shades of the colour blue have no common feature is quite different from the reason why hopscotch and whist have no common features. Shades of the colour blue can scarcely be said to have features at all, other than the feature of being this or that shade of blue. But being a shade of blue (navy blue for instance) is not a feature of navy blue. Since shades of blue have no features it is clear why they have no common features. It is therefore very implausible to suppose that blue is a family resemblance concept. Items which fall under a family resemblance concept do so in virtue of their possession of a series of overlapping features.

Then again, there are many special or technical notions – the concepts of geometry for example – which are quite plainly not family resemblance concepts. The notions of triangle, circle, graph, cos/tan/sin and so on are not family resemblance concepts, though not for the same reason that blue is not. The words 'graph', 'triangle', etc., have precise exact definitions which list the one or more essential properties of a graph or a triangle or whatever, as the case may be. The 'fibres' which make up these concepts, these 'ropes', are in each case as long as the rope itself.

The 'Criss-cross' Description of the Mind

Wittgenstein's own practice in his later works indicates that he thought the best way to answer philosophical questions is to give accurate detailed descriptions of ordinary language, supplemented by descriptions of imaginary languages and 'language-games'. Imaginary languages show what is possible and impossible in our own language, and thereby show us, also, the tightness or looseness of logical and grammatical connections which we otherwise never examine. For example, if we consider the possibility of a language which has no general word for sense-perception we can go on to ask whether individual modes of what we call sense-perception – seeing, hearing, smelling and tasting – are as similar as at first glance they seem to be.

There is good reason for making a sharp distinction between philosophy and science, for science seeks general laws, whereas the differences and distinctions which are embedded in language are manifold and subtle and cannot be captured by generalities. Philosophical problems can be solved only by recognising and describing the conceptual manifold which is created by the infinitely intricate interplay between human languages and human 'forms of life'. So it is in language and the connections between language and forms of life, and not in (for instance) the atomic structures of organic matter, that we will find the fine-grained distinctions that differentiate mental states of various kinds. The difference between, say, hoping one's friend will arrive on Tuesday and hoping one's friend will arrive on Thursday presupposes complex human institutions, including a human language of time, and the fine-grained distinctions between different states of hoping cannot be made without reference to those institutions and that kind of human language. The complex structures of matter which make up brains or computers are manifestations of a different kind of complexity altogether.

The aim of the 'criss-cross' descriptions is to produce a perspicuous view which will first illuminate and then resolve particular philosophical problems. There is no suggestion anywhere in Wittgenstein's later works that this task can ever be completed, and anyway it seems obvious that the manifold of interconnections between human language and human life could never be captured by some huge perspicuous overview. For the manifold is infinitely vast.

Wittgenstein himself, of course, examines in detail a considerable number of psychological concepts, returning again and again to the same questions. He examines common notions such as understanding, knowing, believing, pretending, dreaming, hating, anger, expectation, remembering, hoping, meaning, perceiving. He also investigates less common notions such as 'the feeling that everything is unreal'. He discusses the experience of seeing a picture or diagram first as representing one thing then as representing another (e.g. first an overhanging cornice then a staircase), to which experience (and other similar or related experiences) he gives the label 'seeing-as'. He even writes about the esoteric feeling which a few people have about the 'colours' of the days of the week – Monday black, Wednesday red, Saturday green, etc. He mentions the feeling of *dejà vu* but does not go on to discuss it, because, he says, he never experienced it.

The 'Plan for the Treatment of Psychological Concepts'

A good though small-scale example of the 'criss-cross' in Wittgenstein's philosophy occurs in *Zettel*, where he sets out a 'plan' for an investigation into philosophical psychology. The criss-cross points of this plan include the following.

Psychological verbs are characterised by the fact that statements in the third person and in the present tense are verified by observation, whereas statements in the first person and in the present tense are not.

First-person statements in the present tense are akin to instinctive reactions. (Wittgenstein calls them 'expressions'.) 'I am in pain', for instance, is akin to a spontaneous wince or cry; 'I hate him' is akin to shaking one's fist or frowning.

There are important differences between (1) sensations (e.g. pain, felt heat and cold, itches, nausea); (2) sense perceptions (i.e. seeing, hearing, tasting, smelling); (3) emotions (anger, love, hate, etc.) and (4) cognitive states or attitudes (knowing, believing, expecting, recollecting).

What we think of as modes of sense perception, seeing, hearing, etc., are more different from one another than we suppose: they seem alike because we place them under one term. The differences between seeing and hearing become more apparent as soon as we think about a possible (though imaginary) language which has words for the individual concepts, for seeing, hearing, etc., without having the general term 'sense perception'.

A similar point can probably be made about emotions, sensations and the cognitive attitudes.

What we call 'sensations' have some common features. They all have genuine duration, which means that it is possible to synchronise sensations (two aches, say) and to identify the time or times at which they begin and end.

Sensations have location, yet sensations carry no local signs (unlike photographs). Sensations have degrees of intensity; for example they can be slightly annoying, or just about endurable, or unendurable.

Sense perceptions are capable of giving us knowledge about the world. This is not something that just happens to be the case, rather it is the logical criterion for being a sense perception.

Emotions are not localised. Joy is manifested in facial expressions but it does not occur in the face.

However although emotions have no location in space they do have location in time; they have genuine duration. Emotions tend to run their course, they flare up and die down.

They have characteristic expression-behaviour, for instance characteristic facial expressions.

Emotions are of two kinds, the directed and the undirected. Fear for example is directed at something perceived as dangerous, which may be called the object of the fear. But the emotions of anxiety and depression are not necessarily always directed, they need not have objects.

Emotions differ from perceptions in that they do not give information about the outside world (though they might give information about what the person concerned believes about the outside world).

Sometimes the adjectives applied to emotions really belong to their objects: there is a kind of transference. Thus horrible fear isn't really horrible, it is fear of something horrible.

The *Zettel* plan, or criss-cross grid, is a sort of précis of grammatical and logical distinctions and oppositions which connect, and also distinguish between, the various psychological concepts.

Language and Life

Often Wittgenstein asks: How do we as children learn what anger is? What hope is? What dreaming is? Overall the answer is: By having our spontaneous non-verbal reactions gradually fitted into a linguistic schema by adults, who do this without thinking; and also by our spontaneously imitating the behaviour of adults. But, he says, by behaviour he means behaviour in context. 'For words have meaning only in the stream of life.' He discusses instances of situations in which certain mental states are not possible, drawing attention to the social and linguistic presuppositions which lie behind the meaningful attribution of this or that state to this or that creature.

Here are two examples, hope and remorse:

> One might observe a child and wait until the day he manifests hope; and then one could say 'Today he hoped for the first time'. But surely that sounds queer! Although it would be quite natural to say 'Today he said "I hope" for the first time'. . . One does not say that a suckling hopes . . . and one does say it of a grown man. – Well, bit by bit daily life becomes such that there is a place for hope in it.

> Can only those hope who can talk? Only those who have mastered the use of a language . . . *the phenomena of hope are modes of this complicated form of life.* (my italics)

> Why can a dog feel fear but not remorse? . . . Only someone who can reflect on the past can repent . . . There is nothing astonishing about certain concepts' only being applicable to a being that e.g. possesses a language.

The Private Language Argument

There has probably been more ink spilt over 'Wittgenstein's private language argument' (so-called) than over any other part of the *Philosophical Investigations*. This 'argument' occupies about 20 or 30 paragraphs of the work and there is a great deal of disagreement about what exactly it is supposed to prove and even as to what it is about. The 'argument' is couched largely in rhetorical questions and contains some of Wittgenstein's most striking images – the beetle in the box, the philosopher who keeps a diary of his sensations, the man whose right hand tries to give his left hand money.

Some commentators think the 'argument' is supposed to prove something about language, some think it is supposed to prove something about the following of rules, and some think it is supposed to prove something about sensations.

I have no theory about what Wittgenstein was trying to prove in these paragraphs. In fact I am inclined to doubt that he was trying to prove anything at all. The so-called 'argument' certainly does not look much like an argument. In any case even if he was trying to prove something there is so much uncertainty about what exactly it was that no exegesis by me could be anything but tendentious. All the other exegeses of this 'argument' are pretty tendentious.

Exegesis and Criticism

Until comparatively recently philosophical journals (and books) were full of exegeses of Wittgenstein's works. This flood seems to have slowed down to a large trickle.

Although Wittgenstein has attracted the attention of many expounders and analysers, criticism, especially hostile criticism, has been rare. It is only possible to make guesses as to the reason for this. Perhaps the following have something to do with the matter.

It seems, from memoirs written by Norman Malcolm, and G. H. von Wright and others, that while Wittgenstein was usually admired and often liked, most of his pupils and some of his colleagues were frightened of him. He must have been pretty overbearing. For instance when he taught in Cambridge he introduced his own rules about who could attend his lectures. Norman Malcolm reports that students had to obtain Wittgenstein's permission to attend his lectures, and were asked to give undertakings to come to every lecture of the course and not just to a few. (Turing broke this rule – see *Wittgenstein's Lectures on the Foundations of Mathematics 1939*, ed. C. Diamond.)

I think it will strike most people who read Wittgenstein's own published letters, and the memoirs written by others, that he must have had a pretty anxious and capricious personality. Maybe one effect of this frightening, anxious and wilful personality was to stifle criticism, not only during his lifetime but also for many years after his death. Russell was virtually the only philosopher of importance who knew Wittgenstein well but who nevertheless made some harsh criticism of his (later) work. Norman Malcolm reports that Wittgenstein listened with special attention whenever Russell spoke during meetings of the Cambridge Moral Sciences Club. Wittgenstein respected Russell, and Russell, who was frightened of nobody, was not frightened of Wittgenstein.

More importantly, there is a real difficulty about producing a general criticism of Wittgenstein's later work. For it is hard to see how the results of piecemeal researches can be refuted except by more piecemeal work, by piecemeal objections. There has been some work of this kind but of course it cannot constitute a general critique.

When general critiques do appear they are made up of objections relating to method. Earnest Gellner's book *Words and Things* is a well-known example. Gellner makes no attempt to show that anything written by Wittgenstein is actually wrong. Instead he attacks the presuppositions, and the alleged triviality, of Wittgenstein's method. He also perceives a number of dangerously bourgeois assumptions hidden under the seemingly harmless bed of linguistic philosophy.

Gellner proposes that philosophy would do well to return to grand theory and insists that truth cannot be reached by piecemeal work or by seeking 'the ultimate nuance'. He believes that philosophy must construct large-scale generalisations if it is to succeed in helping us to understand the universe (and society), but he gives no direct argument in defence of this thesis. His argument is indirect and consists in decrying the efforts of linguistic philosophy as such. Yet strange to say he states in footnotes that some linguistic philosophers, though not Wittgenstein, are really quite good after all. The message is therefore rather confused. In my opinion Gellner underestimates the problem of intellectual cloudiness and consequently overestimates the value of large-scale generalisations. He underestimates the value of clarity, and the significance of the connection between logic and language; he also fails to see that some of the most important work of his hero Russell in fact consists of logical analysis of language.

5

Language and Behaviour:
Ryle

Gilbert Ryle's well-known book *The Concept of Mind* is regarded by some interpreters as making a strong case for philosophical behaviourism. But others see his work as a prime example of linguistic and even Wittgensteinian philosophy. I think that Ryle is essentially interested in solving philosophical problems through an analysis of language; on the other hand, his analysis does appear to push him towards behaviouristic conclusions, at least in some degree. Because of the wide influence of his book, and the fact that he is seen as a behaviourist by many interpreters, including some of his own former pupils, the word 'behaviourism' itself has undergone a kind of stretching. Nowadays behaviourism is often thought of as including theoretical conclusions and philosophical methods akin to Ryle's; these however are very different from those of for example Skinner.

Parts of Ryle's book are directed against mistakes which he thinks are incorporated in Cartesian dualism. He describes Cartesian dualism as 'the two-worlds story' and as the theory of 'the ghost in the machine'. Dualism, he say, embodies a *category mistake*.

This concept of a category mistake is a powerful philosophical idea or tool which Ryle explains by means of examples. For instance, we may notice that Smith and Jones are two men and belong in whatever category men belong to, but the Average Man is not a third man, and he or it belongs in a different category.

Bowling and batting are two roles in cricket and belong in whatever category roles belong to, but team spirit is not a third role, and does not belong in the same category as batting and bowling.

Ryle argues that mistakes about the mind come from wrongly believing that mind, like matter, belongs in the category of substance. Thus Cartesian dualists believe in the existence of two substances, material and mental.

Ryle argues that the supposition that there are special non-material mental events and actions which take place in a non-material substance is 'an unfortunate linguistic fashion' which 'traditionally belongs to the two-worlds story, the story that some things exist or occur "in the physical world", while other things exist and occur not in that world, but in another, metaphorical, place'.

He goes on to analyse a fairly large number of psychological notions with the aim of showing that 'mental' items are neither substances nor events. The analyses are intended to show that psychological concepts really fall into one or other of three entirely different categories. These are: dispositions; 'ways of doing or happening' (adverbial concepts); and achievements.

Dispositions

Dispositions include tendencies, abilities, capacities and habits. Several features distinguish dispositions from actions. Actions take place in time ('when') and take time ('how long'). For instance acts of drinking cups of tea frequently take place at about 4 o'clock and generally each such act takes between one and ten minutes per cup. But tendencies to act, that is, dispositions, do not occur at specific times and do not take time in the way that actions and events do.

According to Ryle, states such as knowing, believing, wishing, hoping, fearing, are not deeds but dispositions. This is shown by the fact that it makes no sense to ask how long it takes to believe in God, or how long it takes to know that $2 + 2 = 4$. If someone knows how to play chess this does not mean that a special mental act has taken place in him but rather that he has certain propensities and abilities of which his chess moves are actualisations. The moves are actions but the knowing is not.

Ryle writes: 'When we describe people as exercising qualities of mind we are not referring to occult episodes of which their acts and utterances are effects: we are referring to these overt acts and utterances themselves.' Psychological dispositions are dispositions to perform physical actions (including utterances).

I think Ryle exaggerates here. There is nothing about dispositions as such which means they must manifest themselves in overt acts. Any dispositional account of the mind will be incompatible with Cartesian dualism, of course, because according to Descartes the mind (mental substance) is not a disposition; it is known directly and not via manifestations. But unless it can be shown of each and every psychological disposition that it is ultimately to be fully cashed in overt acts, we are left with the possibility that a non-Cartesian, dispositional, but 'two-worlds' theory might be the true one.

Is it not the case that a disposition may be partly a disposition to think certain thoughts, feel certain emotions, have certain sensations? Its manifestations might themselves be mental items. Take melancholy. There is more to melancholy than getting into bodily states such as tearfulness. The manifestations of melancholy are themselves psychological things. They include emotional states (for instance depression), and gloomy thoughts, and unhappy rememberings, and maybe also nightmares. Each person has his or her own individual sort of melancholic (and euphoric etc.) dispositional manifestations. Not all such manifestations are overt, many are inward and silent.

A PHYSICALIST OBJECTION

Some of the physicalist 'heretics' argued against Ryle's account of dispositions as follows.

The states and structures of physical objects must be the ultimate realities of the Universe. Dispositions and tendencies are derivative and non-ultimate. The reason is that the existence of a disposition requires the prior existence of an underlying state of affairs.

Take for instance the fragility of glass. Suppose we understand the fragility of glass to be one and the same thing as its disposition or tendency to smash when it is struck. Now, this disposition is explained by the fact that glass has a certain particular molecular structure. If glass is made with a slightly different internal structure (toughened glass) it is not fragile.

D.M. Armstrong suggests that any and every proposition of the form 'X has disposition D' presupposes either a proposition of the form 'X has such-and-such a structure' (for permanent dispositions) or the form 'X is in such-and-such a state' (for non-permanent dispositions). States and structures underlie dispositions and explain them, therefore dispositions are less fundamental than states and structures. According to physicalism, the states which underlie the dispositions which Ryle identifies with thoughts, beliefs and so on are brain states. From the proposition that states and structures explain belief physicalists conclude that they just are those very beliefs. The beliefs themselves are simply states of the brain.

It seems to me that even if the existence of a disposition necessarily presupposes the existence of an underlying state or structure it does not follow that the state or structure is identical with the disposition. Being able to run a marathon presupposes that you possess legs, but the ability to run a marathon is not identical with the possession of legs.

Furthermore the thesis that belief is a state or a structure does not seem to square with the fact that anyone, waking or sleeping, at any one time probably has several thousand beliefs, yet no one thinks about all his beliefs at every moment – that would be impossible. Does the fact that everyone has at any one moment several thousand different beliefs mean that he, or his brain, is at any one moment in several thousand different states? This idea seems rather difficult to accept.

Third, it is just as reasonable to explain structures and states of affairs in terms of dispositions as it is to explain dispositions in terms of states of affairs and structures. If glass is fragile that is because of its structure – which is to say that its molecules when arranged in the way they are arranged have a tendency, a disposition, to separate when undergoing shock.

In moving our descriptions and explanations away from 'the capacity of an object A' to 'certain smaller-scale constituents of object A' we shift the question of capacity on to those smaller-scale constituents. In explaining the fragility of glass by its molecular structure we merely bring up the further question of the disposition of atoms and molecules to behave in certain ways when arranged in certain structures. Any explanation of *this* in terms of particles smaller than atoms brings into the picture the dispositions of *those* particles. If the process is finite we are left with some dispositions at the end of the chain, while if it is infinite we can reduce the initial predicate 'fragility' to nothing ultimate at all, let alone a merely structural feature.

It would seem then that dispositions are neither less fundamental than states (or qualities, or objects), nor more fundamental. All these ontological items need each other. Hence there is no conclusion here of an ontological nature that will prove that behaviourism is false.

Adverbial Concepts

Ryle explains the idea of an adverbial concept as follows: '[Sometimes] in describing a person's mind . . . we are . . . describing the ways in which parts of his conduct are managed.' If someone is aware of what he is doing (when eating, say) that does not mean that he is both eating (physical action) and being-aware (mental action); it means only that he is eating in a certain kind of way. Actions can be performed carelessly, carefully, absent-mindedly, as well as quickly, slowly, etc., and Ryle argues that words like 'attending', which seem to name mental actions, should really be construed as disguised adverbs, that is, as similar to words which describe physical actions (e.g. 'quickly'). A person's attentiveness is proved, not by seeking and finding a mental action of attending inside him, but by watching his ordinary physical actions and seeing how, in what manner, he performs them.

Adverbial concepts do not reduce to dispositional concepts. Attending, for example, which is adverbial, occurs in time, unlike believing, which is dispositional. If you read attentively from 4 o'clock till 4.30 then although the attending cannot exist without the reading, still, it goes on for the same half-hour that the reading goes on for. Ryle maintains that one can say *when* Mr N. was attending but not *how long* it took him to attend.

Ryle's idea that attention, heed, awareness, are really adverbial in character seems to boil down to this: the meaning of 'attention' is derived from the meaning of 'attentively', the meaning of 'heed' from the meaning of 'heedfully' and the meaning of 'awareness' from the meanings of such adverbs as 'carefully', 'knowledgeably' and 'deliberately'.

Now, adverbs like 'noisy', 'clumsy', 'jerky' describe perceptible states of affairs, but it is not obvious that adverbs like 'carefully', 'thoughtfully', etc., always or ever refer to anything perceptible. Can one see another person's attentiveness? Is it overt?

It seems that the question as to whether adverbial notions are ultimately to be analysed in terms of overt actions has not been settled one way or the other. I think that the disagreements about whether or not Ryle should be dubbed a behaviourist probably stem in part from the fact that he leaves this question open. It is not clear whether the adverbial account is in itself reductive enough to count as behaviourism.

Achievements

Although achievements occur at particular times Ryle says that they are not actions because they do not *take* time. They are not doings, but end-points. Ryle also calls them 'success-words'. Verbs which refer to achievements and end-points include 'win', 'conquer', 'unlock', 'prove', 'deduce', 'solve' and 'see'. Activities which lead up to end-points can be done well or ill, but the achieving of an end-point cannot be done well or ill because it is not, strictly speaking, done at all. The sorts of actions which lead up to end-points include racing, which if successful leads up to winning; fighting, which can lead up to conquering; and searching and looking, which lead up to finding and seeing. (There are many other obvious examples.)

Yet an appeal to ordinary usage shows that Ryle is wrong here I think. For in ordinary usage it is quite OK to attach adverbs to 'success words'. For example one can win effortlessly, unlock a door illegally, prove a point logically.

In general the idea of a 'success-word' is a useful one. But the fact that mentalistic words such as 'see', 'understand', 'conclude' are success-words does not seem to prove that they must belong in the same category as overt physical behaviour.

Some success-words can refer to achievings which the subject might be unaware of, for instance, a schoolchild might *beat the world sprint record* while running around the playground; or a baby might *regain his birth weight* after recovering from a dehydrating illness.

Some success-words, for instance 'detect' and 'reach', can be applied to inanimate things; electric 'eyes' can detect heat, motor cars can reach 100 miles per hour.

Intuition tells us that neither the baby, nor the car, nor the 'eye' can possibly know that they are succeeding. But that very intuition implies a contrast with cases in which the subject *does* know that he is succeeding. Consider seeing. In a normal adult human being seeing is itself a form of consciousness and to see something is, *ceteris paribus*, a way of coming to know something. Thus some succeedings necessarily involve knowledge or consciousness and others do not. The knowledge or consciousness that distinguishes seeing, hearing, learning and so on from winning, reaching, etc., cannot itself be reduced to physical achievement. In short, the fact that some 'mental' words are success-words does not prove that they function like words which describe purely physical behaviour.

Behaviour, Thought and Belief

Many objections have been raised against Ryle's account of mental notions. Some of these objections misfire; for instance, it is commonly said of him that he tried to analyse *all* mental concepts in terms of dispositions, which is plainly not true.

What is the relationship between statements about behaviour and statements about mental states? This is a question which Ryle never really answers. He often appears to be analysing the latter in terms of the former, yet he also speaks of feelings and consciousness as if they can exist independently of bodily behaviour.

It seems to me that behavioural statements do not in general mean the same as propositions about mental states. They do not even entail such propositions. For behaviour often needs interpretation. That is only partly because there are so many different varieties of behaviour.

When a description of a piece of behaviour requires no interpretation that is usually because the description itself is loaded with mentalistic words. In ordinary life a description in purely bodily terms of facial contours, and arm and leg movements and so on would seem either pointless or opaque. (In ordinary life such descriptions are very rare; they occur mainly in medical diagnosis.)

If someone is shouting and waving his arms about we do not know what he is doing until we can decide whether he is angry, or celebrating, or exercising, or showing off, or whatever. In other words, behaviour is analysed in terms of the mental state, not the other way around. How then can propositions about mental states be reduced to propositions about behaviour?

Another reason why behaviour-statements cannot entail propositions about states of mind has to do with the nature of thought. Ryle says:

> The trick of talking to oneself in silence is acquired neither quickly nor without effort; and it is a necessary condition of our acquiring it that we should have previously learnt to talk intelligently aloud and have understood other people doing so. Keeping our thoughts

to ourselves is a sophisticated accomplishment. It was not until the
Middle Ages that people learned to read without reading aloud . . .
many theorists have supposed that the silence in which most of us
have learned to think is a defining property of thought . . . But
silence, though often convenient, is inessential.

However, what is essential to thought is not silence, but the
possibility of silence. It is not essential to thinking that it should
always be silent but it is essential to the overall notion of thought
that some thoughts are not expressed. In this thinking differs from
reading.

Everyone does have some unexpressed thoughts. This is not a
sheer accident, like the accident that in the Middle Ages people
learned to read silently. For it is not possible to express every single
thought one has, whereas it is perfectly possible to read always
aloud and never silently. In the case of thinking, shortage of time
prevents total expression, for at any one moment one can have
many many thoughts 'passing through one's head' (as we say).
Secondly, many feeling-states are indescribable, which presents a
problem for any philosopher who believes that mental contents are
necessarily expressible. Thirdly, words and sentences can be
numbered, and linguistically competent people know what counts
as one word, as one phrase and as one sentence; but there are no
rules which tell us what counts as one thought, what counts as two
thoughts, and so on. That which is in principle uncountable can
hardly be identical with that which is countable.

That there are such things as unexpressed thoughts is part of the
concept of thought. This is prima facie consistent with dispositional
accounts of the mind, but not with any form of behaviourism that
insists that the 'cashings' of dispositions must be overt physical
happenings. The fact that some thoughts can be silent, and that
overall some *must* be, is I believe sufficient reason to rule out
reductive behaviourism.

Finally let us look at belief. Belief is important in the philosophy
of mind because of its role in ordinary explanations of action, but
also because its complexity makes it resistant to many proposed
philosophical analyses.

A satisfactory analysis of belief must account for all the following.

Some emotions incorporate beliefs by definition. Thus fear
incorporates the belief that something or other is dangerous,
remorse the belief that one has acted badly or wrongly, shame the
belief that there is something about oneself or one's family or
friends which makes one unworthy of respect.

Several mental attitudes can be defined only as varieties of belief. Thus expectation is belief about the future, memory is belief about the past.

Beliefs can be true or false.

Beliefs can be about things that exist, e.g. politicians, and about things that do not exist, e.g. truthful politicians.

Beliefs can be expressed or hidden.

Where p and q stand for propositions, a belief that p is inherently different from a belief that not-p, and from a non-belief, or absence of belief, about p and not-p, and from a belief that q.

It makes sense to say that people hold beliefs when they are not thinking about those beliefs, that is, when they are asleep or when they are thinking about other matters.

Some beliefs are momentary and some last for years.

Theories about the nature of the mind tend to come to grief when attempting to analyse the complex concept of belief.

Any really thorough-going behaviourism must deny the very existence of beliefs which are not expressed in behaviour, but even non-radical forms of behaviourism cannot easily cope with the fact that beliefs need not be expressed.

Behaviourist analyses of particular belief states cannot distinguish ultimately between all such states, because the description of behaviour is less fine-grained than unanalysed propositions about beliefs. Thus the behaviour of Noah expecting a Flood and the behaviour of Noah preparing for a World Cruise will be extremely similar and will overlap at many many points. In order to know what Noah believes about his immediate future we have to ask him to tell us; we need him to speak to us in the unanalysed language of belief.

Part III

French Philosophy of Mind

6

Body and Mind: Merleau-Ponty

Maurice Merleau-Ponty is generally regarded as belonging to the phenomenological school of philosophy. His style of philosophising is fairly typical of that school in that each of his books tends to be about everything. *The Phenomenology of Perception* for instance is not only about perception; it is also about the mind, and the world, and freedom, and space and time, and the *cogito*; and the names of the authors he refers to include Heidegger, Descartes, Husserl, Kant, Hegel and Sartre; also Freud, Koehler and Watson; also various neurologists and physiologists.

However Merleau-Ponty often writes on questions about the nature of the human mind, and what he says about those questions can to some extent be separated from what he says about time, space, the Universe and the *cogito*. His philosophy of mind is embedded in several of his books, and has to be extracted from them; the most important works in this connection are *The Structure of Behaviour*, which is partly concerned with empirical psychology, and the more purely philosophical works *The Phenomenology of Perception* and *The Visible and the Invisible.*

Merleau-Ponty is against Cartesian dualism, that is to say, he rejects the idea of a dualism of substances. On the other hand his theory of the mind could perhaps be called *aspect dualism*. This somewhat rough and ready label links him with the American philosophers Donald Davidson, who I think is an aspect dualist at a linguistic level, and Thomas Nagel, who is a sort of *temporary* aspect dualist. The work of these two philosophers is discussed in chapter 8.

Merleau-Ponty's more detailed discussions about perception and sensation, and especially his discussions of kinaesthetic sensation, contain some surprising echoes of Wittgenstein.

'Le Corps Propre' and 'Le Corps Objectif'

Merleau-Ponty's philosophy of mind starts with the body – perhaps indeed it can best be described as a philosophy of mind-and-body.

His most important thesis about the mind and the body has to do with the unique role of one's own body in experience. He shows the uniqueness of the role not so much by argument as by description, by describing facts which are familiar to everyone but which are not often the subject of theoretical speculation. In this way he can be said somewhat to resemble Wittgenstein, and Oxford philosophers such as P. F. Strawson, who overtly prefer description to theory. But Merleau-Ponty is also different from these men in that his descriptions are often taken from the findings of experimental psychology and from physiology.

In discussing the unique role of the body in experience Merleau-Ponty distinguishes between on the one hand 'one's own body', which he also calls 'the phenomenal body' ('le corps propre' and 'le corps phénoménal'), and on the other hand 'the objective body' or 'the body as object' ('le corps objectif').

The expression 'one's own body' and its French equivalent are very natural and ordinary. However, it had best be recognised that the phrase 'one's own body' intimates possession, and intimations of possession are prima facie philosophically loaded. Intimations of possession hint at Cartesianism, and at what Ryle would call a 'two-worlds theory'. Merleau-Ponty by no means wants to drop that kind of hint.

Experience of one's own body is not essentially experience of an object. It is true that we can and occasionally do experience our own bodies as objects, for instance when we look at one of our own limbs, or listen to our own heart-beat, or feel with the fingers of one hand the pulse in the wrist of the other. And it is possible, too, to *think of* one's body as a physiological entity, as an object which is (of course) physiologically similar to other human bodies. But the role of object is not an essential role for one's own body. One's knowledge of one's own body is typically quite different from one's perception of and one's knowledge of other things. This idea is crucial to Merleau-Ponty's thought.

Transparency, Control, Permanence, Spatiality, Unity

For much of the time and for most of our experience we are not specially aware of our bodies, they are as it were transparent to us. Our eyes are 'transparent' to us, for instance, when we look at things; when we hear sounds we are not conscious of our eardrums – they too are 'transparent' in this sense. When we experience the world our knowledge of our own bodies is in some sense tacit.

The 'transparency' of the sense-organs, the as it were tacit nature of one's knowledge of one's own body, may well explain why Descartes and Sartre ignored the role of the body in experience altogether and were able to think of the human person as *essentially bodiless*. (Merleau-Ponty could have added Locke and Hume and many other philosophers to this list.)

The nature of the command which we have over our own bodies in unique. It is nothing like the command we have over those objects in our vicinity, such as pens and paper, and chairs and tables, which we can command, e.g. move around, by pushing, pulling, lifting, dropping. Our command over pens and tables depends on our experiential knowledge of their shapes and weights, and any command we may have over more recondite objects, such as balloons, soap-bubbles or lumps of phosphorus, depends on our having some knowledge of the physical structures or the chemical constituents of those things. But one's command over one's own body does not depend on knowing anything about its constitution or its weight and size. One's ability to move one's body does not depend on an understanding, even a rudimentary understanding, of physiological processes.

One's own body is also distinguished from objects by its special kind of permanence. The permanence of other objects is contingent, accidental, the permanence of one's own body is not. What this seems to mean is that without the body one could not *be*. Of course it does not mean that a human body exists eternally!

One's own body is further distinguished by its special mobilities and its special spatiality. What this means is that we do not need to locate the parts of our body in Newtonian or Einsteinian space in order to have them at our command. Our command over other physical objects such as chairs and tables does of course depend on our first locating them in space.

One's own body has a special unity, 'la synthèse du corps propre'. Some philosophers have contrasted the simplicity and unity of mind or spirit with the complexity of matter, of bodies. Of course the body regarded purely as a physical object *is* complex, made up of many parts; but it is experienced by normal individuals as unitary. A normal individual in an ordinary situation has no need to look around to make sure all the bits of his own body are still stuck together. Someone who *experienced* his own body as made up of a concatenation of pieces of matter fortuitously linked together would be incapable of movement; he would be very seriously ill. (This proposition is supported by the data of neurology.)

The Body's Interaction with the World

The body is not the blind reactive mechanism depicted by some exponents of behaviouristic stimulus–response psychology.

Because we are not blind reactive mechanisms we do not, and indeed *cannot*, interact with the world around us as if it were merely a concatenation of physical properties. We cannot react to the world without treating it as a more or less meaningful system of situations, contexts and relations. The meaning or significance of the system which makes up the world as perceived by us depends not only on *its* physical properties but also on *our own* biological, psychological, social and cultural properties, and also upon our goals, aims, plans, purposes, intentions, needs and interests.

Carrying out goals, plans and intentions necessarily involves the body. For, as has already been noted, we do not move our bodies as we move objects; on the contrary, our bodies as it were move themselves. Our motor intentions, our intentions to move and to act, are embodied *as such*.

Merleau-Ponty argues that there is no such thing as 'pure thought': thought is conditioned by habit, culture, personal experience and particular contexts, and also by the characteristics of the objective physiological body.

The Interaction of the Senses

According to Merleau-Ponty it cannot be the case that sense-perception and motor skills function separately, nor can it be the case that the different senses function separately from one another. His proof of this rests partly on an examination of evidence from neurophysiology, and includes discussions of normal perceptions as contrasted with abnormal kinds which are caused by mutilations, neural disease, brain damage and so on. Merleau-Ponty, like Wittgenstein, is interested in the philosophical implications of pain felt in phantom limbs.

In the normal human adult all the senses, plus the motor skills, must operate together in a unified way in the subject's exploration of the world. This fact is part of the experienced unity of the experiencing body, described above, but it also accounts for the fact that the world too has a unity for us.

One's body is a natural system of equivalences which translates the information given by the five senses and by our motor abilities into one another. The world, the world as experienced, has a unity which mirrors the unity of the non-objective body, that is, the unity of the complex of sensory and motor potentialities which belongs naturally to the living body. This correlation means that we ourselves contribute structures and meanings to experience, and to the world. Nothing we can know about the structure of the world can be entirely independent of human modes of experience. On the other hand we do not create the world, it is there before we are. Philosophical idealism is false.

It is a tremendously important feature of experience that the perceived properties of objects are not limited to those which can mechanically affect, moment by moment, one or other of the sense organs. Since the operations of the senses and the exploratory movements of the body as a whole are not separate, but intertwined, the perceived characteristics of external objects extend across the senses and beyond the momentarily given. These characteristics mirror our multi-sensory or inter-sensory operations, which are necessarily coupled with mobility, which in turn is of course essentially non-momentary.

Both mobility, and the operations of the senses, presuppose a background.

Thus at any given moment a particular motor skill will be operating against the total background of potential but not at the moment active skills.

Similarly, perception of an object looked at (or listened to or whatever) cannot occur except against a background of other items which may or may not lie in the perceptual field. As an example of the background which does lie in the perceptual field, consider the way in which one can look at a tree, say, and both see and not see the sky behind it. As an example of the background beyond the (momentary) perceptual field, consider the different aspects of the tree which are successively revealed as you walk around it.

We can infer, from the fact that perception cannot occur except against backgrounds of potential movements and potential sensings, that in perception the different senses, and the powers of mobility, must encroach upon one another.

When one is perceiving something at such and such a time or moment, the aspects of the thing which are *not* being perceived at that moment, and which are the correlates or mirrors of what is at that moment potential, that is, the correlates or mirrors of the senses which are *not* being used and of the movements *not* being made – these aspects *somehow have some element of sensory presence*. We see an object, a unified object, we do not see a set of successive aspects or perspectives. We see depth, for instance, and we also see solidity, massiveness. Indeed if we could not see depth and solidity we would not be able to see physical objects as physical objects. We are able to see solidity, etc., precisely because of the encroachment of the five senses, plus the power of movement, upon one another.

The question is not: Do we see the world in depth? But: How is it we can see the world in depth? Merleau-Ponty's answer is interesting in three ways. He answers the question, which incidentally was one of Bishop Berkeley's questions, by reference to the body whose existence Berkeley denied. Secondly, his answer with its account of inter-sensory encroachments appears to be based at least in part on the findings of physiology and of abnormal psychology. At the same time (thirdly) he gives philosophical, a priori and indeed transcendental reasons in support of the empirical surmise that study of the brain will show that the senses – of sight and of touch for example – are functionally and anatomically linked.

Body and Mind

Merleau-Ponty holds that the relation between the body as object (the thing which physiologists study) and the body as experiencing gives us the clue to the nature of human existence and the human mind.

We have two aspects, the mental and the physical, and we should think of the difference between the mental and the physical as analogous to the difference between movement and perception – in other words, as a difference between things which are at the same time indissolubly linked. Just as the visual world in some sense 'contains' the tactile world of mobility, similarly the mental world is somehow 'contained' in the physical world.

One's knowledge of one's own body is to be understood as one's sense of one's bodily mobility and activity and one's ability to interact with the rest of the world. A human mind is a unified collection of bodily skills (potentialities). Such skills are not learnt but are acquired naturally by the (objective) body, they are habitual and open-endedly extendable. It follows from this that a human mind is not a closed system.

The living human body is a physiologically organised entity which has the natural capacity to acquire habitual skills more or less endlessly.   One's own body is the ensemble of these potentialities.

As has already been mentioned, Merleau-Ponty is not a Cartesian. There is only one entity, the body, which however has two aspects. His seeming dualism is a dualism of aspect. In discussing the duality of mind and body he sometimes speaks of a 'dialectic', and a linguistic philosopher might interpret this dialectic as *two ways of talking*, as *two language-games*.

The duality can also be represented through the idea of 'the obverse side'. The phenomenal body is the obverse or other aspect of the objective body.

The mind is embodied in the sense that it can be identified with one aspect of something which is two-aspected. The two aspects are mutually irreducible, and radical behaviourism fails because it tries to bring about an impossible reduction.

The living body possesses a sort of natural ability to acquire habits. It also has a sort of natural ability to find its way around in the world, a natural 'understanding' of the structure of the external world. This is not a conscious or consciously learnt understanding, it is not something which the subject is actually aware of except philosophically or theoretically.

I find a kind of vagueness or incompleteness in Merleau-Ponty's account of the mind. One difficulty is that after describing the supposedly two-aspected character of the person Merleau-Ponty seems to end up with more than two aspects. He seems to end up with more than one obverse or opposite, and it is not clear to me quite which aspect of the person is to be identified with the mind, nor even whether ultimately any identification is intended.

Granted that the mind is not to be identified with all or part of the objective body, is it, then, the same thing as the body's unconscious natural understanding? It seems not, for Merleau-Ponty says that this understanding is something different and more specific, it is not the mind but 'the mind of the body'.

Then is the mind simply 'le corps propre'? If so, does that mean that the mind is to be identified with a collection of perceptual and other bodily potentialities, not (of course) as they are described physiologically, but rather as they are manifested in life? We have to grant that the collection cannot be experienced as a collection; this would conflict with 'la synthèse du corps propre'. We seem to have to say that the mind is a collection which cannot be experienced as that, so cannot be experienced as what it is.

If the mind is a concatenation of capacities it must be a systematic or organised concatenation. This is plain from what Merleau-Ponty says about the intertwining of the motor and sensory capacities. Maybe the mind is best thought of as a system of equivalences which translates the world of sight into the world of hearing, and both of these into the worlds of movement and action and intention – and so on. In that case the mind might be compared to a completely coherent system of maps. According to this metaphor, the map of the seen, the maps of hearing, taste, etc., the map of actual and potential movement and the maps of intention, of projects, of choosing, all overlay one another and each fits on to all the others. And if one map is removed, all the others change. Merleau-Ponty argues that a blind man *feels* the world differently from a sighted man, for instance. A man without a project *sees* differently from one who has plans. Hence the minds of these various people are different.

On the other hand, if we abjure metaphor 'a system of equivalences which organises sensory perception and mobility' looks like a good functional description of the human brain. But the human brain is not an aspect of a two-aspected entity, it is a part of the physiological body, it is part of 'le corps objectif'.

Merleau-Ponty's distinction between 'le corps propre' and 'le corps objectif' somewhat resembles Wittgenstein's distinction between first-person and third-person language (see chapter 4). It also somewhat resembles Thomas Nagel's distinction between objective and subjective reality (see chapter 8). The three distinctions are in my view three aspects of one large metaphysical difference and it seems to me that Merleau-Ponty, Wittgenstein and Nagel all hold that the clue to the nature of the mind can be found lying behind that metaphysical difference.

7

Structuralism: Levi-Strauss

Structuralism isn't really one single theory, it is a series or set of theories, anthropological, literary, literary–critical and philosophical. These theories have in common the general idea that in explaining art or the world it is important to study underlying structures.

Structuralism was originally formulated as a theory about what to look for, and about what could be found, in the study of peoples. As such it is the name of a school of anthropology, yet at the same time (for reasons which I hope will become clear) it is also a philosophical account of the mind.

The inventor or founder of structuralism is Claude Levi-Strauss, a French anthropologist. By 'structures' he does not mean things constructed out of matter but plans or patterns. The concept of structure as it occurs in his theory may be defined as follows:

A structure is a pattern common to two or more systems of classification.

A system of classification is a way of thinking. Examples are the classification of numbers into odd and even, the classification of living things into genus, species and individual, the classification of chemical substances into acids and alkalis and the classification of people into men, women and children.

According to Levi-Strauss there are certain patterns or structures which are common to all human classificatory systems. These patterns or structures are, as it were, the laws of thought for human beings.

Structures in this sense have no special personal features, and no iconic/representational features. They are like abstract maps or grids.

The structures of systems of thought are similar to the structures of languages. Although languages have different vocabularies, there are certain systematic features which they all share. Every language has a grammar. Grammars differ, but only at a superficial level. 'Depth grammar' depends on the human mind, and reveals its fundamental character.

Levi-Strauss says: 'ethnology is psychology'.

In coming to understand the customs of peoples, we at the same time come to understand their ways of classifying things, and this is to understand their minds. Features common to all thought-systems will be common to the whole human race, and therefore will tell us about the human mind as such.

Classification: Proper Names and Logically Proper Names

Readers will be familiar with John Stuart Mill's doctrine that proper names have no meaning, and with Russell's doctrine of *logically proper names*. Levi-Strauss rejects these ways of thinking about names and he specifically refers to Mill and Russell in so doing.

Mill's doctrine is that a proper name as such has no definition, and its connection with the person or thing which it names is arbitrary. A proper name is essentially an arbitrary sound (or written mark) attached contingently to a person or thing by chance or fiat.

Russell's doctrine of logically proper names is as follows.

A logically proper name names something which has to exist both at the time the name is bestowed and also whenever it is used: if the bearer ceases to exist the word loses its meaning, for its meaning *is* the thing it names.

It seems to me that each Russellian logically proper name can have only one bearer. If there were several bearers the name could not be distinguished in a theoretically satisfactory manner from a general name like 'dog'. Let us agree for the sake of argument that every Russellian logically proper name has at least one and at most one bearer.

An ordinary proper name is quite different, it can refer to a dead person, or to an imaginary person, also it can have several bearers.

Before describing what Levi-Strauss has to say about names I shall make a few remarks of a more general nature.

First let's ask: Are logically proper names logically possible?

If names have no connotations, how is the name of one bearer to be distinguished from the name of another?

Either (1) by reference to the bearer itself, or (2) by phonetic features (or scriptive features). But neither method will work.

1   Reference to bearers alone will not guarantee that there is a distinguishably different name for each bearer. If two proper names are to be distinguished from one another by means of the phrases 'the name of this' and 'the name of that' it is perfectly possible for both names to sound and look like 'Smith'. But then logically proper names will not be any different from ordinary proper names in respect of uniqueness.

2   Reference to phonetic or scriptive features cannot guarantee that a proper name has only one bearer. It is impossible to know for sure, i.e. to verify or falsify, whether a particular sound or mark on paper has been, is, and will be, connected to only one item in the universe. If I name my cat, or my sense-datum, with what I hope is a logically proper name, say 'Grurglepudding', I cannot be sure that another cat-owner or sense-datum-owner living in the Congo, or in the future, will never give his or her cat or sense-datum the same name.

Perhaps we should think of logically proper names as *limiting cases* of names. Limiting cases can be specified, and here Russell has given us the specification.

There seems to be no general reason why limiting cases cannot be produced as well as specified. Unless there is some good reason against producing logically proper names wouldn't philosophers have produced some? If they are not produced that may be because like round squares and married bachelors they do not exist.

Philosophers discussing logically proper names do not produce any. They are content to use such formulae as:

'Let N = any logically proper name.'

Here N functions as a variable, not as a name.

Russell himself suggested, semi-jokingly I think, that the pronoun 'this' is the only logically proper name. But that word obviously doesn't fit his specification.

PROPER NAMES PROPER

Against Mill and Russell Levi-Strauss holds that the giving of proper names can never be arbitrary but on the contrary is always determined by rules. Proper names can themselves be classified and because of that they classify their bearers, at least implicitly.

He remarks also that names almost always exist long before the individuals who bear them.

Names belong to functional systems and sub-systems. If the words (sounds) which we call *names* did not belong to rule-governed systems, they would not be names at all.

I shall illustrate Levi-Strauss's point with a few examples.

If someone decides to call his cat 'Fido' he expects the name to be treated as a kind of joke. If everyone in the Philosophy Department is called 'Bruce' that also is a joke. The jokes arise because unformulated rules have been broken. When Russell suggested that the word 'this' is a logically proper name he did so in a characteristically semi-joking way: after all, a pronoun cannot be a name!

In Western nations virtually everyone has a first name and a surname. The surname is functional, it passes to the individual from his father (or mother) and shows what family he belongs to. The acquiring of a surname follows certain rules. Of course in Western nations in modern times changes and variations are permitted. Variations – which are also sometimes disguises – can be produced by the individual when grown up (as in the cases of Ernest Saunders, Richard Sylvan), or by parents for their infants (as when people give their babies new hyphenated surnames).

Even invented names have to follow a positional rule. For instance 'Judy Chicago' means something rather different from 'Chicago Judy'.

Christian nations used to have lists of approved first names, mostly taken from the Scriptures. Every child had to have a name from the approved list; it was illegal to give a child an invented first name. The custom of limiting possible first names to a traditional collection is strong even in places where the law has been abolished or never existed. A binary classification of first names into male and female is one obvious feature shared by traditional collections and less traditional naming practices.

(On the other hand it has to be admitted that in Northern America the rules surrounding the first-naming of children are becoming more and more fluid. In that continent naming is starting to edge closer to the philosopher's paradigm.)

In India and Nepal names are indicators of caste. Caste cannot be disguised if one retains one's family name.

Names everywhere are a resonably reliable indicator of race and nation, though the practice of bankers, ex-spies, criminals and entertainers of disguising their origins or choosing more glamourous labels tends to complicate this. On the other hand, the disguises would not work so well if there were not typically English names, typically Polish names, typically upper-class names, typically proletarian names and so on.

A Russellian objector might argue that these are systems which only *happen* to exist. Surely they don't *have* to exist? Couldn't someone make up an entirely new word, and then name his child or his cat or his house with that word? Wouldn't that be a case of giving a name by fiat, and wouldn't the name be a logically proper name?

One could indeed make up a new word and name some person or thing with that word. However it isn't in anyone's power to prevent the new word from slipping into the existing system. As soon as it acquires a bearer it will begin to work inside a pre-existing system. If the new word is to name a person it will be treated according to the grammatical and social rules which govern personal names; for instance in a Western society it will be treated as a surname or a first name or a nickname but probably not as all three at once. In India it will become a caste indicator. Everywhere it will be made to follow any positional rules there may be in relation to other names, or to titles and other designations attaching to the named individual.

It is perfectly possible to make up a new word and bestow that word on an individual with the intention that it should become a proper name. This often happens when animals are given names. But we must not confuse the arbitrariness which characterises the *bestowing* of the name with an arbitrariness of *use*. If the use of the word were to be arbitrary it would not be a name, or a word.

Even in naming, viz. that area of language where philosophers have tended to see no system but only arbitrariness and random choosing, there is in fact much system, and many rules both formal and unformulated. This I believe supports Levi-Strauss's thesis that all thinking rests on classificatory systems. It is not in our power to think without systems.

Levi-Strauss's thesis is also of course supported by his work on other less general and maybe less familiar classificatory systems.

Classification: Species and Totems

The most notable totemic peoples are (some of) the Aboriginal tribes of Australia, and (some of) the Indian tribes of North America.

A totem is a natural object, usually but not necessarily an animal, fish or bird, which is taken as an emblem of a people or a clan, and which appears in the myths of the people in various supernatural roles, including that of Creator of the Universe, and mystical progenitor of a race or clan.

At first glance tales about people being descended from bears, eagles, badgers, kangaroos and so on look like a kind of superstition indicating considerable ignorance of well-known facts relating to human and animal reproduction. And it seems that some early European observers of primitive peoples in Australasia and the Americas really regarded totemism in this light. These observers thought that totemism must be a kind of pre-scientific way of explaining things that we in the West can explain more successfully with our science.

This was a naive view, not consonant with common sense. It was always prima facie likely and is indeed the case, that totemic peoples themselves understand perfectly well that human beings are never begotten and conceived by bears and kangaroos and other non-human animals. They believe that the 'descent' of the human group from the totemic animal is as it were a mystical descent. The totem stories are in some sense metaphorical.

But what is the meaning of the metaphor?

Are totemic tales just fairy tales which the people tell little children to amuse them? This cannot be the answer. Totems are associated with important rules about peace and fighting, and marriage, and general socialising, and food, and other things as well. Some of the rules are extremely strict so that violation is punished by death.

Totemic descent is used to divide a people into groups whose social relations with one another are defined by prohibitions and injunctions of various kinds. For instance, it is generally the case that a man cannot marry a woman who has the same totem animal as himself. In other words, if a man is said to be 'descended' from a certain animal then he cannot marry a woman who is perceived as having originated *from the same source*. Because of this Freud argued (in *Totem and Taboo*) that the implicit function or purpose of totemism is to prevent incest.

Freud and Levi-Strauss are in agreement in holding that totemism is not meaningless superstition. Primitive man is not more mystified or more inherently mystifiable than modern man. He is not 'lost in a maze of confusion'. We are mistaken if we think primitive people are less rational than we are. They know less, or know different things, but they are not less rational.

Levi-Strauss agrees with Freud that totemism has social functions or purposes, and he also agrees that its purpose is not to explain natural causes. Totemism is not pre-scientific science (as it were). Freud held that the social purpose of totemism is to justify and to enforce the prescription against incest but Levi-Strauss considers that it has a much wider function. Indeed he thinks it is used in different ways in different communities, he does not believe it is one single phenomenon; and therefore he sometimes speaks of 'totemism so-called'. (However for convenience I shall use the word 'totemism' without the adjective.)

Totemism provides ways of classifying people and things. The 'structures' found in the thought-systems of primitive man do not radically differ from those found in the thought-systems of modern man. We have to remember of course that by 'structures' Levi-Strauss means the formal features of systems of classification. The elements of the different systems may differ greatly from one another. It is those differences which seem to distance us from primitive man, and which partly explain why we fail to see the similarity between his thinking and our own.

Primitive man constructs systems of classification out of elements or materials very different from the ones found in the classificatory systems used by modern man. But primitive logics, like our own, are shaped by human beings who insist on *differentiation*.

Primitive logic is based on *observed* contrasts, often binary contrasts, in the qualities of concrete objects both natural and manufactured. Our systematizing, our logic, on the other hand, rests on *non-concrete* contrasts (which are also often binary) – for instance odd/even, positive/negative, plus/minus, squares/square roots, true/false and so on. However there are traces of 'concrete logic' in some Western customs. Heraldry displays a kind of concrete logic for instance. Still, speaking generally, concrete contrasts are not part of the patterning grids of modern thought but rather emerge from them.

Totemistic categorising uses a selection taken from the various species of non-human animals as grids. These grids are always used in the first place to classify human beings, into races, nations, clans and families. They may also be used to classify the rest of nature, including such items as the winds, the sea and so on; and sensory qualities; and even non-concrete items like the points of the compass.

It is an essential part of Levi-Strauss's thinking that these or those animals, plants, artefacts, colours, etc., can have quite different roles in the thought-systems of different peoples. Hence there are no 'natural symbols' of the kind presupposed by some Freudians, no Jungian 'Archetypal Ideas' and no such thing as a 'collective unconscious mind'.

It is only forms (structures), not contents, which are common characteristics of human minds. Both in practice and in theory the *existence of differentiating features* is of much greater importance than the *particular features as such*.

It is easy enough to prove the first point with examples. I shall mention only a few.

For us black is the colour of mourning and white the colour of weddings. In China white is the colour of mourning and red is the colour of weddings. In Europe priests and monks wear non-chromatic colours, in Asia they wear red, orange and yellow. In some totemic systems (according to anthropologists) the Sun figures as a kindly father, in others as a people-eating beast which will one day burn us all up. In some societies certain foods are regarded as dangerous, in others those same foods might be regarded as especially delicious and perhaps reserved for royal persons (pork in Israel, pork in Fiji).

To return to totems.

Levi-Strauss says that totemic classifications are both *thought* and *lived*.

The operative value of systems of naming and classifying stems from their formal character, not from content; they are like codes. This is true of totemic systems of classification as much as it is of our own non-concrete logic.

One of the central functions of these codes is to enable people to move from one realm of thought to another. Totemic codes mediate between natural facts (the different characteristics of different animal species) and cultural institutions (the social differentiations which constitute kinship groupings, marriage laws, leadership, feuding and peace, property divisions, etc.).

Classification: Totem and Caste

As an example of Levi-Strauss's ways of arguing that different classificatory systems exhibit similar structures or patterns we can look at what he says about totem and caste.

Totem and caste are two opposite-seeming methods of classifying human groups.

Totemic classificatory systems are used by exogamic peoples who do not exchange manufactured or other inanimate goods in an unrestricted fashion.

Caste is endogamic and belongs to peoples who exchange very various goods and services with one another.

However, this is a somewhat simplified picture, for Levi-Strauss believes that no peoples are completely endogamic, since this would allow incest, and according to him incest, though variously defined, is universally forbidden. He believes that in varying degrees all peoples are partly 'endo' and partly 'exo'. Indeed, there are societies (he gives a few examples) which have both caste and totem. The existence of such societies is one of the reasons why he thinks totemism is not a single phenomenon.

Nevertheless even extreme cases of totemistic and caste societies respectively have similarities. Their thought-systems, their classificatory systems, have the same patterns or structures. Caste and totemism are inverse methods of classifying the world and human experience. They are opposites which exhibit the same basic forms. One is just the other turned inside out. The structural identity between occupational castes and totemic groups is an inverted symmetry.

Thus: In Hindu India different castes have different special tasks: only Brahmins can be priests, Rajputs are soldiers, the merchant caste has innumerable subdivisions according to the things it makes and sells, and the Harijans or outcast people have to do all the really disgusting jobs. Inter-caste marriage is still strongly forbidden by custom in modern India. In other words, Hindus are strongly endogamic.

Differentiation is essential to human thinking. Castes taken collectively are heterogeneous in function. A caste society gets its needed differentiation by strongly differentiating between different social and work functions. The diversity of function, though created by human beings, is of course real and not imagined, that is, different kinds of work really exist in the institutionalised world, the world of human cultural reality. The inanimate products of the work of the different castes are exchanged between the castes through commerce and in other ways. Caste society, having made its differentiations along these lines, can recognise that human beings, who are produced naturally and not by work, all belong to the same species, in other words, there is no need to deny that human beings are as it were *undifferentiated*. This mental grid pertaining to the caste system allows endogamy. But at the level of ideology a strong differentiation then latches on to the real (though indeed institutional) differences between different kinds of work and social function. These real differences acquire a significance which in a sense is imaginary in that it is ideological. Endogamy becomes not merely allowed but necessary, that is, it becomes necessary to forbid marriages between people whose groups do different kinds of work. Otherwise there would be *too much* differentiation, what Levi-Strauss calls 'an accumulation of functions [which] . . . is of no practical value'.

Differentiation is essential to human thinking. Totemic societies differentiate strongly between types of human beings; at the level of ideology and the imagination they perceive human beings as 'descending' from different animal species. These differences, of course, are not real: different human families do not belong to different species. Just as caste systems exchange genuinely different inanimate things unrestrictedly but do not exchange people (women), so totemic societies exchange people but do not unrestrictedly exchange things. Foodstuffs, for instance, which are derived from plant and animal species which are differentiated in the world of reality, cannot be exchanged unrestrictedly in a totemic society because of the totemic injunctions and prohibitions governing the eating of your own totemic animals and plants.

Edmund Leach's Objections

Edmund Leach in his critical book about Levi-Strauss says that he himself has 'a personal prejudice' in favour of trying to discover the details of how particular societies work rather than looking for large general similarities between them. Yet at the same time some of Leach's own writings have a definitely structuralist bent.

Leach's criticism of Levi-Strauss's work is an attack on structuralism but it is not confined to structuralism.

One of his first objections is that Levi-Strauss's anthropological fieldwork, which was carried out in South America, is 'of only moderate quality'. He goes on implicitly to deny it any quality at all, for he says that Levi-Strauss chose to ignore 'the standard research techniques' of modern anthropology (which involve e.g. learning the languages of the peoples being studied) in favour of making generalised descriptions based on information taken from local interpreters and from the books of earlier writers. Levi-Strauss spent relatively little time with the peoples he was studying and in his works on myth and kinship he even describes peoples he has had no contact with at all.

Leach also says that Levi-Strauss's work on kinship systems is vitiated by his mistaken assumption that all descent systems are unilineal.

Another criticism is that Levi-Strauss is 'a visionary . . . and the trouble with those who see visions is that they find it very difficult to recognise the plain matter of fact world which the rest of us see all around'.

Leach objects too that although Levi-Strauss constantly affirms that the structures of primitive thought are the same as those of modern thought he never actually demonstrates this. And at the same time, he says, Levi-Strauss holds that modern societies are not suitable subjects for anthropological investigation anyway because they are not static.

Leach complains that the translations of Levi-Strauss's books from French into English contain ambiguities especially when the translations were by the author himself.

He objects to Levi-Strauss's references to 'the human mind' ('l'esprit humain') and would prefer the term 'the human brain'.

Leach explains structuralist accounts of thought systems by giving a structuralist account of traffic lights. This looks very much like a spoof.

In general Leach seems to think that Levi-Strauss's structures are imposed *ad hoc* on the evidence, such as it is.

On the other hand he believes that Levi-Strauss has succeeded in demonstrating that the processes of food preparation and the categorising of foodstuffs according to their various methods of preparation are elaborately structured in all societies. He believes that Levi-Strauss has probably produced enough evidence to prove the universality of the hierarchical structure called 'the culinary triangle' which is associated with the status of different ways of preparing foods.

Finally, Leach says that since the human brain is roughly similar in all races of people it is not unreasonable to suppose that there may be similar patterns underlying the manifold cultural differences to be seen in mankind. The only problem is that Levi-Strauss has not proved that the structures are what he says they are.

It seems to me that ethnological structuralism contains two elements.

The first element is the thesis that all races of humanity and all human societies create classificatory systems which are of course structured in some sense. Now, no one seriously believes any more that there are any human societies which lack language, or which do not make classifications, or which live 'in a maze of confusion'. It is agreed by everyone that human beings are creatures who categorise their experience and use symbols to do this.

The second element is the thesis that, although classificatory systems differ, their underlying structures reflect the character of the human mind as such and are therefore the same in all races and societies.

If there are structures of thought everywhere but no structures common to all classificatory systems it would seem to follow that the characteristics of the mental systems of individuals are either personal or culture-dependent.

Leach's main point is that the patterns and structures to be seen in human life and thought cannot be proved to be universal.

Perhaps from the point of view of the philosophy in mind it is what structuralists and semi-anti-structuralists such as Leach have in common that is important. Both sides agree that the mind can best be explained by finding out *what it does*, and they agree that what it most importantly does, because of its very nature, is create classificatory systems.

This outlook contrasts with that of philosophers (physicalists and functionalists) who are not interested so much in what the mind does but rather in how it does it. Clearly it is necessary, if one wants to find out *how* the mind works, first to know something about *what it does*. In ordinary life functionalists and physicalists of course know about many of the wonderful products of the human mind but when philosophising they sometimes appear to be ignorant about what the 'it' is that the mind can do. A strict diet of Anglo-American functionalism can create the impression that the most important workings of the human mind consist in operations like seeing red patches and believing things about cats on mats.

Part IV

Mind, Science and Explanation

8

Varieties of Dualism

Most philosophers understand by 'dualism' a dualism of substances. Ryle for instance argues against dualism by attacking the notion of the ghost in the machine. Skinner and Armstrong both assume that the only kind of dualism possible is a dualism of material and mental substances and events.

However there is more than one kind of dualism. Or perhaps we will avoid begging any questions if we speak here of pluralisms instead of dualisms.

There is the pluralism of the separate sciences, of types of explanation, of solipsism versus other minds, of symbols and their meanings, of 'wide' and 'narrow' mental states, of subject and object. These pluralisms are not inconsistent with a dualism of substances, but, on the other hand, they do not compel us to accept a dualism of substances either.

The purpose of this chapter is to examine some of these pluralisms.

The Pluralism of the Sciences

It will be argued in chapter 10 that some of the separate sciences are autonomous. If this is correct then even if one day it became possible to translate the statements of all sciences into those of physics there can be no ultimate reductions *which retain explanatory power*. In other words, the statements when translated into those of the supposedly ultimate science would cease to explain and would therefore cease to perform the function of scientific theories.

One way reductionists can avoid this conclusion is to draw up and defend a narrow definition of *science*. If it turns out that botany, or economics, or cosmology, cannot be reduced to the favoured science of physics it is at least prima facie open to the reductionist philosopher to argue for the view that these 'soft' sciences are not really scientific after all.

Pluralities of Description: Donald Davidson's Anomalous Monism

The American philosopher Donald Davidson is a physicalist who believes in a monism of substance and a sort of dualism of description. He calls his theory *anomalous monism* and its main features are as follows.

Mental items can be defined by a special quality which Davidson, following Brentano, calls 'intentionally'. Intentionality is a property of mental states whereby they can have contents which need not correspond to anything in the material world. Thus the mental state of holding a false belief about the material world does not correspond to anything actually in the material world.

In spite of this feature of mentality, in spite of the intentionality of the mental, it remains the case, according to Davidson, that mental characteristics are nevertheless only special types of physical characteristics. They are characteristics of the brain. Mental characteristics are also 'in some sense dependent, or supervenient, on physical characteristics'. (Note here Davidson's pre-Kripkean conception of identity which allows him to equate identity with dependence and supervenience.)

The theory of anomalous monism is explained by reference to three principles which are apparently but not really inconsistent with one another. These are:

1 the Principle of Causal Interaction. This is that at least some mental events cause physical events and vice versa.
2 the Principle of the Law-like Character of Causality. This states that wherever there is causality there must be a causal law.
3 the Principle of the Anomalism of the Mental. This principle states that, because of the intentionality of the mental, there are no laws which enable us to predict or explain mental events.

Although the three principles taken together appear to yield a paradox Davidson argues that the paradox can be removed.

His way of removing the seeming paradox is to argue in effect that we have two kinds of vocabulary. One vocabulary can be used to formulate scientific laws, the other is radically unsuitable for making law-like statements. The second vocabulary is the one that we use in our ordinary talk about mental events, and it is permeated, as it were, by intentionality.

When mental events and mental characteristics, which are really brain events and brain characteristics, are wearing their intentional/mental labels, they cannot be fitted into law-like statements and therefore cannot be predicted or explained via causal laws. But that fact is quite consistent with mental events actually being causes or effects of physical events. The Principle of the Law-like Character of Causality only means that

When two events are cause and effect they have *some* descriptions that instantiate a law.

It does not mean that

Every true singular statement of causality instantiates a law.

Causality and identity are relations which hold between individual events however described. But the laws of science are linguistic. Therefore events can *instantiate laws* only if those events are described in an appropriate way.

Events can be *explained or predicted via causal laws* only if they are described in an appropriate way.

The Principle of Causal Interaction is 'blind to the mental–physical dichotomy' because it deals with events described non-intentionally. The Principle of the Anomalism of the Mental 'concerns events described as mental, for events are mental only as described'. These principles are therefore not in conflict with one another or with the Principle of the Law-like Character of Causality.

I have to confess to a feeling that Davidson's reasoning is rather fuzzy.

Why does he say that laws are linguistic? Are they any more linguistic than, say, definite descriptions of individual events? Why does he say that events are mental 'only as described'? Are events also 'physical only as described'?

Although Davidson does not think it is just an accident that we have this way of talking about mental events, he does not explain in this paper why the vocabulary of intentionality is so important, and he does not really explain why mental events cannot be predicted. If some mental event E really is identical with some physical event P, and if the physical event P falls under a causal law and can be predicted, how is it that a different label, E, renders the event unpredictable?

Davidson's theory rests on the idea that we have pluralisms of description. Now, pluralism of description does not entail pluralism of explanation. However the intentional language of the mental is explanatory as well as descriptive. Davidson's theory has room only for causal explanation, so that, unless he holds that explanatory mentalistic concepts are not explanatory at all, he owes us an account of how intentionality is to be reconciled with causation between particular events.

He also owes us an account of the relationship between causal laws, which he says are linguistic, and the causal relation between particular events, which he implies is not.

If linguistic pluralism is indeed irreducible there might be more to it than a feature of language. It could be argued that there is something in our experience which forces a certain kind of language upon us, which forces us to describe beliefs and other mental items in intentional terms. That something need not be a ghost in a machine.

The Pluralities of Explanation: Causal Explanations

Causal explanations are not all of one kind. Some explain individual events, some explain classes of events, some explain how things work, some explain how things begin.

Explaining how things begin, and explaining individual happenings, generally both involve a reference to antecedent events, as in these examples:

'What caused your injuries?' 'I was run over by a cyclist.'

'Why does this rat refuse to run in the left-hand maze?' 'Professor Skinner gave him an electric shock every day last week whenever he tried the left-hand maze.'

'How does tinnitus begin?' 'It generally begins after the subject has undergone the experience of prolonged loud noise such as gunfire.'

Explanations of how things work generally take the form of descriptions of sequences of events. Consider for example the answers which are given to questions like: How does the heart work? How does a motor car work? How does an electric bell work? How does the solar system work, that is, what do the sun and the planets and the moons of the planets *do*?

In the first three examples the sequences of events whose descriptions constitute explanations are repetitive. They can be seen as chains made up of antecedent causes whose effects then become causes whose effects then become causes . . . and so on. In the fourth example this isn't the case. The state of the solar system on Monday isn't the cause of its state on Tuesday. Some explanations of systems are really just descriptions of what happens, thus the behaviour of the solar system is 'explained' by describing the paths of the planets. Even though there is no mention of antecedent causes in this description it has always been regarded as a completely respectable scientific account.

Pluralities of Explanation: Logical Entailment and Covering Laws

The covering law model of scientific explanation is associated with the philosopher Carl Hempel. I shall give only a very brief account of his theory here because it is discussed again in the next chapter.

According to Hempel a proper scientific explanation consists of three parts: a law statement, or universal generalisation of the form *whenever an event of type TX happens an event of type TY happens,* a statement of particular conditions of the form *event EY has happened*, and a statement of the subsequent conditions or happenings of the form *event EX has happened*.

Hempelian inferences are deductive; Hempelian explanations are logical entailments. As such they are different from ordinary commonsensical causal explanations.

Pluralities of Explanation: Explaining Concepts

Much teaching consists in explaining concepts. For instance, in order to teach someone the rules of cricket you have to explain among other things the concept of Outness, the meaning of being Out. You have to describe what it is to be bowled out, run out, caught out, out leg before wicket and Not Out. (Explaining concepts nearly always involves answering tricky subsidiary questions: for example, if a batsman skies the ball and then catches it himself, is he Out or Not Out?)

Take another example, teaching astronomy. I have never attempted to teach anyone astronomy, nor indeed to learn it, but one can see that it must involve explaining some exceedingly abstruse notions, for instance the concepts of gravity, relativity and anti-matter.

As to mathematics, apart from providing practice in computation the teaching of pure mathematics must consist almost entirely of explaining concepts.

Explaining concepts is not like explaining beginnings, or causal connections, or how things work, nor is it like making deductive inferences.

Pluralities of Explanation: Explaining Actions

In every human language (I believe) there exists a vocabulary which is used to explain the actions of human beings. This vocabulary is the language of knowledge, belief, desire, emotion, intention, purpose and long- and short-range planning. It is not used by modern peoples to explain the behaviour of inanimate matter except in phrases like 'the selfish gene' which one *supposes* must be intended as metaphors.

The vocabulary of action–explanation is largely intentional. The truth-value of a statement about a belief (and so any explanation in terms of someone's beliefs) does not depend on the truth of statements about the physical world. Thus 'Tim believes there are mermaids' can be true or false independently of whether or not mermaids actually exist. For this reason explanations in terms of beliefs, desires, hopes, etc. differ radically from explanations in terms of (say) force, mass, velocity, action and reaction.

The vocabulary of belief and other mentalistic concepts is not only used for explaining what human beings do, it can also be used, in a restricted way, to explain at least some of the actions of the other higher animals. For instance anyone who has ever met a few horses will know that they are creatures which have strong likes and dislikes for particular human beings and for other horses, they also often have marked character traits such as friendliness and laziness. There are many occasions on which it is perfectly natural to explain a particular horse's more aggravating actions in terms either of his character traits or his likes and dislikes.

Some philosophers have suggested that the explanatory language of belief, pain, knowledge and so on will one day be replaced by a more scientific language that will refer only to physical items like molecules and brain cells. This suggestion is usually accompanied by an unargued assumption that there can be genuinely different kinds of explanation only if there are genuinely different kinds of entity. Richard Rorty for instance writes:

> The discovery of a new way of explaining the phenomena previously explained by reference to a certain sort of entity, combined with a new account of what is being reported by observation-statements about that sort of entity, may give good reason for saying there are no entities of that sort. The absurdity of saying 'Nobody has ever felt a pain' is no greater than that of saying 'Nobody has ever seen a demon' if we have a suitable answer to the question 'What was I reporting when I said I felt a pain?' To this question the science of the future may reply 'You were reporting the occurrence of a certain brain-process.'

There are two comments to be made on this.

The first is that not all nouns refer to entities. The relevance of this point can be seen from the following example:

Explaining the concept of a limit, as this occurs in the differential calculus, is not like (say) explaining how vaccination prevents smallpox. It is a different kind of explanation altogether. It will be agreed, I suppose, that it would be not just rash but positively stupid to predict that one day science will produce a new kind of 'suitable answer' to the question 'What did I mean in the past when I talked about a limit?' For the answer we have now to that question is perfectly sound. But the soundness of our present explanation of the concept of a limit does not mean that a limit is after all a special kind of *entity*. The second comment is that the ordinary language of belief and desire shows no signs of withering away in the face of discoveries in physics, chemistry and neurology. One cannot so much as imagine trying to do without ordinary mentalistic explanations and descriptions. Rorty is maybe talking about replacing the irreplaceable.

Pluralities of Explanation: The Non-transitivity of Explanation

Some relations are transitive, some are intransitive and some are non-transitive.

Thus the relation 'ancestor of' is transitive, i.e. if X is Y's ancestor and Y is Z's ancestor then X must be Z's ancestor.

The relation 'spouse of' is intransitive, given that pairs of spouses are always of opposite sex. So if in a polygamous or polyandrous society A is the spouse of B, and B is, as well, the spouse of C, A cannot be the spouse of C.

The relation 'half-brother of' is non-transitive. It is possible but not necessary, when A is B's half-brother and B is C's half-brother, for A to be C's half-brother.

The relation between an explanation and what is explained is non-transitive.

Explanation can be described either on the linguistic plane or on the plane of facts. Explanation can be thought of as a relationship, either between statements, or between states of affairs, as the case may be.

For instance, when explaining meanings we sometimes say 'This statement is an explanation of that one' and when explaining how things begin or continue or how they work we might say 'These facts explain those facts.'

Let us compare explaining meanings with making translations. It seems to me that the relation 'is a perfectly accurate translation of' is a transitive relation between statements, so that if p is a perfectly accurate translation of q and q is a perfectly accurate translation of r then p must be a perfectly accurate translation of r.

However the possibility of perfectly accurate translation is a moot point in itself. Ordinary translation is non-transitive, like the visual indistinguishability of shades of colour. When shade s1 is visually indistinguishable from shade s2, and s2 from s3, and s3 from s4, it need not be the case, though it can be the case, that s1 is visually indistinguishable from s4.

Explanation of meanings is somewhat similar to ordinary as against impossibly perfect translation. If one statement translates or explains a second, and the second translates or explains a third, and the third a fourth (etc.), it need not be the case, and indeed rarely is the case, either that the first statement in the series can by itself explain the last, or that it is a good translation of the last.

Now let us consider an explanation of a fact in terms of other facts. Suppose someone asks

1   'Why is it that this small bamboo table can support the weight of 16 books without collapsing?'

And suppose this question leads to a series of answers as follows:

2   'Well, bamboo is a much stronger wood than you might think from its appearance.'

3 'And that is partly because it is hollow and partly because of the character of the cells of bamboo wood.'

4a 'And hollow wood is stronger than solid wood.'

4b 'As to the cells of bamboo wood, they have such-and-such a molecular structure.'

5a 'And cells with such a structure also have certain other features, namely . . .' [etc.]

5b 'And hollow wood is stronger than solid wood because . . .' [Here follows a description of the weight-bearing features of hollow things.]

In the example it can be seen that, while 2 explains 1, and 3 explains 2, and 4 explains 3, and 5 perhaps explains 4, it does not follow that 5 explains 1.

Is the non-transitivity of explanation the result of its intentional character, its mental character? Certainly explanation requires understanding, an explanation which does not lead to understanding is a failure.

Should we be looking for an ideal explanation or an ideal understander?

Perhaps for an ideal understander the last in any series of explanations would always suffice by itself to create understanding of all the other explanations in the series, and of the original question. For him, or Him, since He could only be God, all explanation would be both transitive and superfluous.

Conversely the ideal explanation would be so simple and so lucid that any creatures capable of understanding at all would come to understand the why or how of the original question as a result of hearing it. I do not know whether the ideal explanation would be transitive, intransitive or non-transitive. Perhaps it would have to be unitary, like Berkeley's account of the seeming manifold of causes as being nothing in reality but a collection of signs plus One First Cause.

Since explanation is non-transitive, except perhaps for those whose powers of understanding are infinite, the possibility of reducing one explanation to another cannot ever be guaranteed. Still less can it be guaranteed that different kinds of explanation can be reduced all to one kind. In other words, the hypothesis that there is one unitary system of explanation of the whole of reality is not well supported.

Explanations anyway come from human minds whose powers we know are not infinite. Why should it be assumed that there could be such a thing as a total explanation of reality?

Methodological Solipsism and the Dualism of 'Wide' and 'Narrow'

Methodological solipsism – the term is Carnap's – is described by Hilary Putnam as 'the assumption that no psychological state, properly so-called, presupposes the existence of any individual other than the subject to whom that state is ascribed'. (In fact, the assumption was that no psychological state presupposes the existence of the subject's *body* even: if P is a psychological state then it must be logically possible for a 'disembodied mind' to be in P.)

The assumption, says Putnam, is 'pretty explicit in Descartes, but it is implicit in just about the whole of traditional philosophical psychology'.

As is evident from Putnam's description, methodological solipsism is a restrictive programme which deliberately limits the scope and nature of psychology to fit certain preconceptions. Historically these restricting preconceptions have been Cartesian and mentalistic, having stemmed from Descartes' programme of philosophic doubt.

However modern physicalist and functionalist accounts of mentality also carry the restrictions of methodogical solipsism.

Physicalism holds that mental states are brain states. Naturally such brain states may have external causes, but it is generally agreed that it is always in principle possible to describe an effect without reference to its cause. Hence physicalism has to assume that mental states can be fully described without reference to the world outside the individual.

The case with regard to functionalism is complicated by the ambiguity of the word 'function'. However neither definition of 'function' allows an escape from the restrictions of methodological solipsism. If a mental state is (as Lewis holds) whatever mediates as a causal factor between input and output then, given the same assumption as above, namely that effects can be described independently of their causes, it follows that mental states can be described without reference to anything outside the individual whose mental states they are. A similar conclusion follows if we take a function to be an analogue of a mathematical function. There is nothing about a mathematical function which necessitates its having any particular interpretation and so nothing about it which necessitates a reference to the world outside the individual.

Those who abjure methodological solipsism do so on the basis of the difference between 'wide' mental states, such as belief, fear and regret, which carry references to the world outside the thinking subject, and 'narrow' mental states, such as pain, objectless depression and so on.

The point is not that 'wide' mental states are caused by states of affairs outside the individual. They might be or they might not be so caused. The point is that such states *presuppose* states of affairs outside the individual. Presupposition, of course, is a logical relation, not a causal one.

'Narrow' mental states, on the other hand, which also might or might not have external causes, carry no presuppositions about states of affairs outside the individual.

The difference between the 'wide' and the 'narrow' can be illustrated with examples of the former, such as jealousy, regret, gratitude, hope, fear and so on.

If you confess that you are jealous of y you normally believe that y exists, contrary to any solipsism. Emotions like regret, gratitude and vengefulness presuppose the existence of a past containing human relationships, while the mental stages of hope and fear presuppose external benefits and external dangers and a real world existing outside the solipsistic self.

In short there are not a few mental states which presuppose the existence of objects, states and relationships existing independently of the mind, brain, body or Cartesian soul of the person who has the states. Methodological solipsism only permits accounts of narrow mental states and therefore makes it impossible to include ordinary everyday mental states like jealousy, regret, belief and expectation in a philosophical theory of the mind. These perfectly ordinary mental states have to be in some way reconstructed if the assumption of methodological solipsism is retained.

Attempting such a reconstruction makes sense only if one has adopted yet another highly restrictive methodological assumption, the assumption that every occurrence of every type of wide mental state is based on a profound illusion. This is a heavy and pointless theoretical burden to have to carry.

The Dualism of the Schematic and the Iconic

Since methodological solipsism is incompatible with the existence of ordinary mental states such as belief and jealousy it also rules out the possibility of the uniquely personal element in mental states like memory.

The uniquely personal character of memories is vividly described by the physician Oliver Sacks in his essay 'Reminiscences' in which he describes the experience of his elderly patient Mrs O'C. Mrs O'C. was born in Ireland but left for America at the age of five after being orphaned. She had never returned to Ireland. In her eighties she suffered a stroke which caused her to 'hear' a continuous 'concert' of Irish songs and melodies, and this 'concert' produced memories of her mother's singing and the feel of her mother's arms around her.

Sacks relates how the studies of Wilder Penfield located the origin of musical hallucinations in epileptic people in the seizure-prone points of the cerebral cortex by electrical stimulation of those points. Penfield thought that such hallucinations were lost memories but believed that their recollection was essentially meaningless and random. On this Sacks seems to disagree. He writes:

> Stimulate a point in the cortex of such a patient, and there convulsively unrolls a Proustian evocation or reminiscence. What mediates this, we wonder? What sort of cerebral organisation could allow this to happen? Our current concepts of cerebral processing and representation are all essentially computational . . . and as such, they are couched in terms of 'schemata', 'programmes', 'algorithms', etc. . . . But could schemata, programmes, algorithms alone provide for us the richly visionary, dramatic and musical quality of experience – that vivid personal quality which *makes* it experience? The answer is clearly . . . 'No!' . . . a gulf appears between what we learn from our patients and what physiologists tell us . . . the mind [is] 'an enchanted loom' [with] patterns of meaning which transcend purely formal or computational programmes or patterns, and allow the essentially *personal* quality which is inherent in reminiscence, inherent in *all* mnesis, gnosis, and praxis . . . above the level of cerebral programmes, we must conceive a level of cerebral personal scripts or scores . . . Experience is not *possible* until it is organised iconically; action is not *possible* unless it is organised iconically.

Everyone's thoughts and memories have the features described by Sacks, that is, they are iconic, they represent a real or imagined world outside the thinker's head, and they are personal.

The problem here, which cannot be solved by anyone who adopts the stance of methodological solipsism, lies in the difference between programmes and patterns on the one hand, and representations of personal experience on the other. There must be serious difficulties involved in trying to reduce the personal and particular to what is essentially general and law-like, and these difficulties cannot be removed simply by dwelling on the variety of uses possible for the word 'representation'. The 'solution' offered by the retort 'But surely chemical and physical processes can represent things? Don't the rings on a tree represent its age?' seems to me to be no better than a pun.

The Dualism of Subject and Object

In 1971 Timothy Sprigge argued that the essential condition of consciousness is that there must be 'something it is to be like' such and such a person or other creature. Thomas Nagel took up this point in 1973 when he asked 'What is it like to be a bat?'

We understand that our perceptions are caused by physical things and physical phenomena (such as light and sound) acting on our sense organs.

We also believe that one and the same thing can cause very different perceptions in different people or on different occasions.

What is more, it is only common sense to hold that one and the same thing produces different perceptions in different species. It is only common sense to believe that physical objects which human beings detect with their eyes must seem very different to bats, who detect things not only with their eyes but also with something akin to radar. It is only common sense to believe that things which look thus and so to us must look pretty different to spiders, whose eyes are constructed differently from ours, and to eagles, who can see mice moving from distances of hundreds of yards, and to fish whose eyes are on the sides of their heads; and so on.

The qualities of perceptual experiences go to make up part of 'what it is like to be this particular person' and also part of 'what it is like to be a creature of such and such a type'.

The perspectival view perceived by an individual located at this or that point in space differs somewhat from those of other individuals nearby, and it differs more markedly from those of human observers further away. So there is something which it is like to be *this* human being standing at *this* point in space with *these* normal or colour-blind eyes looking at those and those physical objects in such and such a type of sunlight or moonlight or electric light or whatever.

There is also something more general which we could call 'what it is like to have typically human perceptual experiences, what it is like to see things in space, and from points in space, as human beings see them'.

Materialist philosophies of mind rest on the fundamental principle that the whole of reality can be described in objective physical terms. The physically objective world is the only world there is, and it exists independently of subjective human or animal perspectives. According to materialist philosophies how the world seems to this or that person or animal has little if anything to do with what the world really is.   Nagel challenges this principle in his book *The View from Nowhere*.

He describes the physical conception of reality as follows. Common sense, and materialist philosophy of the reductivist type, both say that underneath the different appearances of things there must lie a reality which is independent of how things appear to us or to any other animals. The world would exist even if there were no human or other observers in it, hence its true nature must be detachable from how it seems to human or other observers. Materialist philosophy of the reductivist type holds that this true reality is the whole of reality. Common sense, however, probably regards the detachable part of true reality as incomplete.

According to materialist/reductivisit philosophy, if we wish to reach a conception of the world as it objectively is we have to *not* think of it from an individual point of view or perspective, and *not* think of it from a general human perspective. The physical world as it is in itself contains no points of view and nothing that can appear only to one particular point of view. Whatever it contains can be apprehended by a general rational consciousness divorced from the particular sensory organs of particular individuals or species.

Although this conception of objective reality has been immensely useful in the development of physics it cannot be the whole story. The subjective perceptual points of view which are left out of the objective account continue to exist, furthermore they are the necessary conditions of our acquiring evidence about the physical world. We cannot collect evidence except from where we are in space and time and since we have to have positions in space we have to have a perspective. We cannot get any view of the world at all unless we have sensory organs. The objective conception of the physical world is itself formed by mental activity, by philosophers and scientists thinking about sensory evidence, space, time, other species and so on. A complete explanation of reality will have to take account of these things for they too are part of reality.

Well, can the mental phenomena of sensory experience and thinking be analysed as themselves part of physical reality?

Nagel says that behaviourist, physicalist and other similar reductions of mind to matter are bound to fail: 'The subjective features of conscious mental processes . . . cannot be captured by the purified form of thought suitable for dealing with the physical world that underlies appearances . . . mental states – however objective their content – must be capable of manifesting themselves in subjective form to be in mind at all.'

We tend to think of the physical no-perspective conception of reality as objective, and of the mentalist, perceptual, perspectival 'as-it-seems-to-observers' conception as essentially subjective. Nagel however believes that we need to develop a conception of *mental objectivity*. The reasonable part of physicalism (and similar theories) is not its unitary and reductionist approach but rather its apparent or partial success in giving some kind of an account of objectivity. We should consider the possibility of 'a less impoverished and reductive idea of objectivity'.

Nagel insists that mind, like matter, is a general feature of the world. In the case of mind as well as matter we as individuals are all in fact acquainted with many examples in our own small spatio-temporal neighbourhoods.

However, before we can assert this we need to refute scepticism about other minds. Scepticism about other minds stems in part from that very feature of minds which makes them special, the fact that minds apprehend the world in an essentially perspectival manner. Since, according to the sceptic, I know all about my own perspective but nothing about yours, I have no solid reason for believing in the existence of your mind. Of course I *can't help* believing in it all the same. But that is instinctive belief, according to the sceptic, not rational belief.

Nagel, following P. F. Strawson (an Oxford mentor), argues that understanding that there are other minds entails having a general concept of *subjects of experience*, a concept which one can and does place onself and other human beings under, just as one places all trees under the general concept of *tree*.

Although there is a general conception of mind that allows us all to believe in the existence of other minds, its acquisition is regarded by sceptics as highly problematic. For other people appear to us as physical objects in the material world, not as subjects of experience.

Still, we cannot abandon the essential factor of a point of view when thinking about the minds of others; it is impossible to think of other people – still less of ourselves – as simply material objects existing in non-perspectival space.

Nagel says here that we can and do arrive at an objective conception of mentality simply by *generalising the idea of a human perspective*. There is no more difficulty about generalising the idea of a human perspective than there is about generalising the idea of some object like a table. And surely he must be right in this. After all we are well able to generalise all kinds of ideas. We can generalise the idea of colour, and kinship, and shapes and species, and we also generalise difficult abstract notions like space and time. We easily generalise ideas related to *geometrical* perspective.

It seems to me that the supposition that we cannot achieve a general idea of the subjective confuses the content of an idea with its use and its acquisition. The idea that an objective concept of the subjective is impossible is not more plausible than the idea that it is impossible to have a rational definition or explanation of irrationality. Arguing that an objective concept of the subjective is impossible is rather like arguing that the word 'nothing' can have no meaning. Just because the concept of mind involves the notion of subjectivity, and hence is in some sense tied to that notion, it does not follow that it is restricted to what we can understand in terms of our own individual experiences. Such a restriction would prevent the concept of mind being a concept at all.

Is objective reality – that is, objective physical reality plus objective mental reality – all that there is? To this question Nagel answers 'No'. For part of reality is not only subjective but particular. It is natural for us to generalise such ideas as the idea of the human perspective, the perspective of bats, and perspectival experience as a whole. But these generalised and objective notions cannot (as Nagel puts it) tell me what scrambled eggs actually taste like to me. The content of experience is particular. It is undoubtedly part of reality. So objective reality is in some sense incomplete. There is more to reality than the objective and the generalisable.

Is Nagel a crypto-Cartesian? I don't think so. Indeed, he does not see the reality of the subjective as a basis for any kind of dualism. For Nagel the dualism of the objective and the subjective is *temporary*.

He writes:

What is needed is something we do not have: a theory of conscious organisms as physical systems composed of chemical elements, and occupying space, which also have an individual perspective on the world, and in some cases, a capacity for self-awareness . . . In some way that we do not now understand, our minds as well as our bodies come into being when these materials are suitably combined and organized. The strange truth is that certain complex biologically generated physical systems, of which each of us is an example, have rich nonphysical properties. An integrated theory of reality must account for this . . . if and when it arrives, probably not for centuries, it will alter our conception of the universe as radically as anything has to date.

And 'Why should the possession of physical properties by the body not be compatible with its possession of mental properties – through some very close interdependence of the two?' (Perhaps, as Spinoza believed, the properties are ultimately the same, but that would have to be at a deeper level than either the mental or the physical.)

This seems to reflect a deeply anti-dualist stance, the stance of Neutral Monism. Nagel believes in the theoretical possibility of obtaining a unified theory, albeit a theory which will need a new and enlarged conceptual scheme. Just as the phenomena of electricity and magnetism could not be explained in purely mechanical terms but needed a shift to an enlarged theory incorporating the new concepts of electrodynamics, so a unified theory of mind and matter can only be achieved when the uniqueness of mental phenomena is recognised and new concepts constructed to take account of it.

9

The Study of Matter and its Laws

Materialist theories of mind rest on two hypotheses or assumptions which are that theoretical knowledge as such is ultimately unitary, and that physical science as we have it now, though not necessarily complete, nevertheless forms a basis for a unified body of knowledge. The philosophy of linguistic analysis, on the other hand, perceives theoretical knowledge as including more than science and certainly more than physical science. Finally, it can be seen from the examples of French philosophy discussed in Part III that opinions about which sciences count as relevant to philosophy are liable to differ from one nation to another.

The Scientific Paradigm

It is said that we live in an age of science. What does this mean? Well, for one thing, it means that there are far more professional scientists living and working now, all over the world, than there ever have been before. However the present high profile of science is not due only to numbers, but rather has to do with influence and prestige. The ultimate reason for the current widespread prestige of science is probably economic.

Scientific discoveries and advances in technology are taken to be the paradigms of truth and knowledge, if not by everyone, then at least by large numbers of people in the West, including (of course) most scientists. Admiration for science can turn into anthropomorphic superstition, as in the case of a schoolboy whose words were reported in a letter to a newspaper in 1985. He was asked if he believed that God made the world and replied 'No – Science made the world.'

Can science and scientists themselves decide whether nor not science is the only form of real knowledge? Science, as Nietzsche remarked, does not investigate itself, but the rest of the world. Although a scientist, like anyone else, might well hold philosophical theories which can be rationally defended as philosophy, science *per se* does not deal with questions like What is science? What is knowledge? And it is far from obvious that the methods of science are themselves appropriate for objectively examining the claim that those very methods are valid and extendable paradigms which other enquiries should emulate.

Philosophy (on the other hand) has always asked abstract questions like What is truth? What is knowledge? It is surely one of the functions of philosophy to ask abstract questions, not incidentally as a way of getting somewhere else, but as a central concern. This role is a better one than the role of handmaiden to other subjects. In the past, in the West, when philosophy was regarded as the handmaiden of religion, it performed its handmaidenly task by explaining and developing the teachings of the Christian church without criticising them. Similarly, nowadays philosophers mostly seem to believe that philosophy should be allowed to make only very benevolent comments about physical science.

In this century philosophy has also concerned itself with the status and respectability of other disciplines, and, it has to be admitted, it has sometimes made a fool of itself in so doing.

Still, philosophy can at least formulate the right questions even if it sometimes gets the wrong answers.

The question as to what is genuine and what is pseudo-science should not be confused with the question as to what is real knowledge. For the definition of science is both too elastic and too narrow to allow science to count as the only paradigm of knowledge.

Defining Science

What is science? Every school in the philosophy of science gives a different account of what science is. In addition there are the accounts given by scientists themselves, by politicians, by schoolteachers, by media men and by the general public. Science has not so far been given a clear definition which everyone agrees about. There is disagreement about its subject-matter, and disagreement about its methods. The only methodological rules which nearly everyone would agree are essential to science are extremely general and very banal: 'respect the evidence' for instance.

We may get some insight into this matter if we take a brief look at the history of the word 'science'.

Until the nineteenth century the word 'science' could be applied to any branch of theoretical knowledge or learning. Since then, however, it has increasingly come to refer only to those branches of knowledge which have to do with the material universe. Science now is the science of matter.

At the same time, scholars working in other branches of knowledge have persisted in referring to their own subjects as sciences – examples include anthropology, economics, linguistics, philology and psychology. These scholars call their subjects sciences because they believe that the methods used are 'scientific', that is, intellectually respectable. 'Scientific' and 'science' are very much Hurrah Words. Hence pure mathematics is often described as 'scientific', even though its methods are not experimental. All that can be meant is that pure mathematics is an intellectually respectable discipline.

The word 'science' comes from the Latin verb *scire* = to know. The senses listed by the OED as still in use are:

1 Knowledge as a personal attribute. Example: 'Though we have not science of it [the supernatural] yet we have . . . powerful presentiments' (Seeley, 1882).
2 Mastery of any department of learning. 'Those seeds of science called his ABC' (Cowper, 1781, on the alphabet).
2a Trained skill, e.g. horsemanship, pugilism.
3 A particular branch of knowledge and study, a recognised department of learning. In the Middle Ages 'the seven sciences' were the seven liberal arts, viz. Grammar, Logic, Rhetoric, Arithmetic, Music, Geometry, Astronomy.
3b Contradistinguished from art. Science is then equated with theoretical knowledge and art with practical knowledge, i.e. with knowledge of the methods for obtaining certain results. But 'science' can also mean a department of practical work which depends on the application of theories or principles. Here the distinction from 'the arts' means that the latter are seen as dependent only on traditional knowledge and skills acquired by practising or through habit or unconscious learning
4 A branch of study concerned either with a connected body of demonstrated truths, or with observed facts systematically

classified and more or less colligated by being brought under general laws, and which includes trustworthy methods for the discovery of new truths within its domain. This definition allows the inclusion of many different subjects including pure mathematics, anthropology, economics, linguistics, philology, psychology.

5   The kind of knowledge of which the various established sciences are examples. In modern times this is often restricted to the kind of knowledge supplied by the natural or physical sciences, excluding pure mathematics and the sciences of mankind such as ethnography and philology.

Since about 1860 the word 'science' has usually meant physical and experimental science, that is, the study of matter and its laws. Science is the systematised knowledge of matter and its properties. The OED notes:

> The many conflicting systems proposed in recent times and the need frequently arising (apart from any formal classification) for a common designation applicable to a group of sciences that are related by similarity of subject or method, has given currency to a large number of expressions in which the word 'science' is qualified by an adjective . . . Amongst the more prominent of the adjectives designating particular classes of science are *abstract, concrete, biological, physical, exact, descriptive, experimental, historical, mathematical, mechanical, moral, mixed, pure,* and *natural*.

The use of these adjectives creates classifications or groupings of the sciences which overlap deeply at many points.

'Matter and its Laws'

When considering science defined as 'the study of matter and its laws' we perhaps need to remember that *matter* is not a completely unproblematic notion.

First, the contents of the material universe are not all of them easy to observe in an unproblematic way. It may be that chairs and tables are easier to detect than minds and souls but chairs and tables are not the constituents of the universe as studied in physics and chemistry. Atoms and electrons have no qualities capable of being directly perceived by the senses. They are known to us only by the series of events in which we suppose them to be implicated. We know about them by observing chemical reactions, or by watching tracks in cloud chambers, or by 'looking' at them with electron microscopes. Second, developments in modern physics have led some scientists to conclude that physics might actually be incapable of providing a conception of *what is really there independent of observation*. Physics might be unable to give an observer-free picture of the ultimate constituents of the universe. This is because quantum theory cannot be interpreted in a way that permits the phenomena to be described without reference to an observer.

The Philosophy of Science: Carl Hempel and the Deductive Model

Hempel's theory is that scientific inference is essentially deductive. He holds that the scientist begins by observing empirical facts, such as the fact (e.g.) that a spring will stretch when a weight is attached to it. After many observations have been made a covering law is postulated. A covering law is a universal generalisation of the form 'Whenever an event of type TX happens an event of type TY happens.'

The scientist, having discovered his covering law, constructs a scientific explanation of events which consists of three parts:

1 a statement of the relevant universal law;
2 a statement of particular conditions of the form 'event EY has occurred';
3 a statement of the subsequent happenings or conditions of the form 'event EX has also happened'.

As an example let us imagine that the scientist happens to be Robert Hooke and the covering law Hooke's Law of the Spring. Hooke's Law of the Spring states that the increase in the length of a spring when a load is attached to it is always proportional to the weight of the load. (We need not bother whether this is in fact a true law.)

According to the deductive model, Hooke, or anyway an idealised Hooke, after discovering his Law would thenceforth reason as follows when confronted with events involving springs:

1 The increase in the length of a spring when a load is attached is always proportional to the weight of the load.
2 Here is a spring whose length is x inches, and now I attach a load of y pounds to it.

3   The increase in the length of the spring is (or will be) a function
of x and y.

The covering law model of scientific explanation as stated above
cannot cope with statistical inference, but it was modified by
Hempel in 1962 in order to do just that.

Hempel believed that all scientific explanation worthy of the
name, including all explanation of human action, must take
the form of inference involving covering laws. Non-Hempelian
explanation is either incomplete, or not genuine explanation at all.

The model has certain weaknesses one of which is that, even
when it includes the 1962 modifications, it does not cover all types
of explanation of physical events. The demand that proper
explanation must include reference to covering laws rules out many
ordinary explanations. Consider for example the following dialogue:

'Why was there a fire at the hotel?'
'The owner wanted to beat the planning laws and bribed someone
to commit arson.'

There are no covering laws – not even statistical ones – to explain
all fires in hotels, nor any laws to cover all cases of bribery and
arson. We cannot say 'whenever a hotel owner wants to beat the
planning laws he will bribe someone to commit arson' or 'whenever
a man is offered a bribe he will take it' nor 'all hotel fires are due
to arson'. Yet in spite of the absence of any relevant covering law
there is nothing 'unscientific', that is, nothing irrational, about the
explanation of the fire as given.

Overall the Hempelian model depicts the progress of science as
cumulative, consisting of fact collection and theory formation
supplemented by the removal of old theories when newly discovered
facts cannot be accounted for by them. Small-scale laws are gradually
replaced with more general ones which cover more and more of
the facts, and when older theories are retained for particular
purposes they are represented as specialised forms of newer ones.
For example Newton's laws, which are still used for terrestial
calculations and moon-shots, are often depicted by science writers
as if they were actually consistent with Einstein's theory.

These overall features of the Hempelian picture have been
recently criticised by two other philosophers of science, Thomas
Kuhn and Paul Feyerabend.

Philosophy of Science: Thomas Kuhn

Kuhn argues, from historical evidence, that science does not progress by accumulation. He also argues that methodological directives, of which Hempel's model is one type of example, cannot dictate unique answers to scientific questions.

Kuhn distinguishes two kinds of science: 'normal' science and 'revolutionary' science.

He holds that normal science, which is everyday science, is a type of empirical investigation which presupposes the truth of current theories and treats these as paradigms. Normal science proceeds by determining known facts with more precision, by investigating unexplained facts with the aim of trying to explain them in terms of existing theory, and by resolving ambiguities in accepted theories. In short, says Kuhn, normal science proceeds by trying to force nature into the currently accepted theoretical–conceptual boxes.

In the absence of a paradigm all the facts that could possibly be relevant to some particular question or area of enquiry have to be regarded as equally relevant. But nature is intricate and vast; hence pre-theoretic fact-gathering is close to random and is far less important in science than Hempel's model suggests. Observation must limit the range of admissible scientific belief but it is equally true that observation itself must be severely restricted before questions can be posed in answerable forms.

The restriction of observation is brought about by a number of factors, including the invention of special apparatus designed for very specialised purposes, but the main restriction is imposed by existing theories or paradigms. If need be fundamentally novel discoveries will be suppressed either until normal science has invented some suitable apparatus, or until such time as a scientific revolution occurs.

Normal science research problems have little to do with making new discoveries or producing novel theories. Quite often everything except for one small esoteric detail in the result of an experiment is known in advance. The researcher is solving the puzzle of the one esoteric detail. (Kuhn compares normal science with solving jig-saw puzzles.)

Nevertheless normal science makes constant progress. This is because the paradigm theories of the day are the criteria by which the scientific community decides what are the possible areas of research, what constitutes genuine science, *and what counts as progress*. Normal science owes its huge success rate to these facts, which ensure that scientists choose solvable puzzles to work on.

Paradigms are not methodological rules. Scientists only start to think about methodological rules, and to refer to them in discussion, when a theory which has served as a paradigm looks like being inadequate after all.

Very occasionally there is a scientific 'revolution'. This happens when existing theories become unsatisfactory for some reason or another. For a time there may be several rival theories floating around.

Two things determine the success of a theory over other rival theories. In the first place it must solve a few problems the other theories cannot solve and it must look like solving more.

In the second place it must be supported by a group of scientists who for one reason or another are able to compete successfully with other groups of scientists who support the rival theories.

What enables some scientists or scientific groups to compete successfully with their rivals? Superior intellectual ability is not the whole story. The reasons why one group is able to compete successfully with others might well include such factors as money, social prestige or popularity, unscrupulous use of research material, powerful political friends and so on.

If Kuhn is right the process of theory elimination as described by Hempel, Popper and others is a fiction.

Normal science, which means most science, follows paradigms and presupposes the truth of existing theories. Creative or revolutionary science is a comparatively rare process which leads to the overthrow of old theories and paradigms and the institution of new ones. Scientific textbooks then describe the old theories either as non-scientific, that is, as magic, superstition, religion, etc., or (on the other hand) as simpler, more specialised versions of current theories.

Neither of these ways of representing old scientific theories is correct, says Kuhn. Old theories are not magic, they are not unscientific, and they really do conflict with newer theories (and other older ones).

Textbooks also standardly speak of current theories as if they were the final truth on the matter, with no room for anything new after now. Yet in fact old theories sometimes come back in new forms, no science is static, and no science is without anomalies which conflict with current theory.

Kuhn thinks that the suppression of historical fact and the

distortion of the nature of scientific enquiry to be found in science textbooks is necessary for the training of scientists. It is necessary, he says, for the young scientist's mind to be closed off against theories which are not productive at the moment.

Neither normal science nor revolutionary science is anything like the picture of science which appears in science textbooks. And, even more strange, the 'methodological rules of science' described by famous philosophers completely fail to describe correctly science as it actually is. What is the explanation of this failure?

Kuhn thinks the explanation is that philosophers of science are taken in by reading science textbooks. Science textbooks set out current theories and findings as final truth. Philosophers of science then articulate the logic of science *as it is described in the textbooks*.

The false idea that science has a natural unity can also be traced back to science textbooks. The idea of the unity of science rests on the (probably unconscious) supposition that science is going somewhere. It resembles a theological belief in the destiny of mankind, a belief that underneath the multifarious plans of humanity there lies an ultimate purpose. The idea that science is somehow aiming at one final Truth is similar also to the belief, held by pre-Darwinian evolutionists, that the evolution of species has an intended end-point, chosen by God or Destiny. Science is indeed somewhat similar to the natural species that have evolved on earth in that it grows constantly in intricacy, articulacy and specialisation. But it is not going anywhere, it is not going towards some final end or ultimate Truth.

Finally, Kuhn argues that different branches of science, and different areas inside one branch, use different theories and different paradigms, and there is rarely very much overlap. Even when a single theory overlaps two or more branches of, say, physics, it is interpreted differently, and is given different weight, in the different branches. The kind of 'unity' manifested in such case is no unity at all.

Science turns out not to be the monolithic and unitary enterprise it looks like when viewed through the writings in textbooks, but 'viewing all fields together, it seems instead a rather ramshackle structure'.

Philosophy of Science: Epistemological Anarchism

Paul Feyerabend is even more radical in his approach to the question: What is science? To begin with, he thinks that there is no such thing at all as a general scientific method. The creative scientist, whatever his theoretical opinions on method, in practice adopts the slogan 'anything goes'. Not even a commitment to the empirical evidence is a necessary part of successful scientific research.

> there is no 'scientific method'; there is no single procedure, or set of rules that underlies every piece of research and guarantees that it is 'scientific' . . . Every project, every theory, every procedure has to be judged on its own merits and by standards adapted to the processes with which it deals. The idea of a universal and stable method that is an unchanging measure of adequacy . . . is as unrealistic as the idea of a universal and stable measuring instrument that measures any magnitude, no matter what the circumstances. Scientists revise their standards, their procedures, as they move along and enter new domains of research. The main argument for this answer is historical: there is not a single rule, however plausible and firmly grounded in logic and general philosophy that is not violated [by scientists] at some time or other. Such violations . . . were necessary for progress . . .

Feyerabend, like Kuhn, argues by producing historical evidence, taking as his two main examples Galileo, and the development of quantum theory. (There is no room in this book to reproduce Feyerabend's detailed historical material: readers should consult the Bibliography for further enlightenment.)

> Science is not sacrosanct. The mere fact that it exists, is admired, has results, is not sufficient for making it a measure of excellence. Modern science arose from global objections against what went before . . . rationalism itself . . . arose from global objections to commonsense. Are we to refrain from engaging in the activities which gave rise to science and rationalism in the first place? . . . Are we to assume that everything that happened after Newton (or after von Neumann) is perfection?

There are no rules or standards which determine the structure of research in advance. On the contrary, every piece of research is simultaneously a potential instance of the application of a rule and a test of that rule. Research has a dynamics of its own, it can proceed in the absence of clear rules, it can suspend rules. Nobody can anticipate new ideas and new solutions and nobody can say which rules will be suspended or when: the human mind is endlessly inventive and responds to unforeseen problems with unforeseen solutions. Even the rule that empirical evidence is of primary importance in empirical science is often inapplicable, because what counts as a fact, and hence as evidence, is always partly determined by the nature of one's existing theories, including those 'silent' theories which are embedded in common sense. A new theory makes one interpret the evidence differently, or leaves the scientist and his theory for the time being with no supporting facts. Sometimes theory takes precedence, sometimes evidence does: much progress in science is made up of *ad hoc* moves. Science has many anarchistic features and often takes leaps into the void.

Science is standardly described as more logical, more self-critical and more rational than other activities. But what (asks Feyerabend) does such praise amount to? What standards of rationality are being invoked?

One standard which is explicitly invoked by scientists and philosophers of science is the standard of consistency. But (Feyerabend argues) the idea that science proceeds by trying always to be consistent is false. The criterion of consistency, if seriously adhered to, would mean that the first adequate theory invented would have the right of priority over any equally adequate later theory which did not fit in with the first one. Alternatives to an accepted, entrenched theory could be countenanced only if they shared its confirming instances. This would lead to total stasis. In fact innovative scientists do not and could not proceed like this: but many people, including many scientists, think they do. Also, when scientists, even innovative scientists, get old and stultified they appeal to consistency as a way of defending their own outmoded notions.

Refusal to consider new theories which are inconsistent with old ones has the effect of eliminating potentially refuting facts, facts which could refute the old theory. All such potentially refuting facts will then either be explained in terms of the old theory, often with the use of *ad hoc* assumptions ('epicycles'), or, if the worst comes to the worst, will simply be ignored. There are many cases of facts being quietly ignored until something turned up to explain them. Sometimes nothing has turned up yet, but the theories in question are accepted all the same.

Pluralism of theories and method is internally essential to science. Feyerabend calls this stand 'epistemological anarchism', the theory that 'anything goes', that no ruling out or ruling in of theory or fact can be advocated in advance of the appearance of the (inevitably unpredicted) new problems that constantly appear. Science would first ossify and then cease to exist if the open-ended pluralisms of explanation and methodology which make up science as it actually is were to be abandoned because of the official though unused rules of procedure which scientists wrongly believe underlie their practices. Feyerabend goes even further and argues that it is important to accept a wider pluralism still, an external-to-science kind of pluralism. Science needs outside or external tests or checks as well as internal pluralisms. But where can such checks come from?

There are two possible sources. One is the study of the history of science, that is, the study of theories which are now thought to bé false. These older theories are often condemned by modern scientists as 'magic': nevertheless, what is abused as magic in the twentieth century is even so historically a part of science. (Feyerabend repeatedly accuses scientists and philosophers of culpable ignorance of the history of science.)

The second kind of intellectual test or check available is to be found by looking at current procedures which have been condemned as unscientific by the scientific establishment. Examples are chiropractice, osteopathy, herbal medicine, acupuncture. Feyerabend thinks it is a sign of intellectual decadence, and indeed of self-seeking chauvinism in modern scientists that they are happy to condemn *without examination* the medical and agricultural practices of so-called primitive peoples, and of 'untrained' people working unofficially in their own community, and to condemn *without examination* such practices as voodoo, astrology and so on. It is not that osteopathy and voodoo are necessarily all right, what is at issue is scientists' willingness to condemn them before examining them, contrary to the often-vaunted 'open-mindedness' of science.

A truly critical and self-critical approach in and to science would involve accepting the possibility of both internal and external pluralisms of explanation. It would entail a general unwillingness to condemn past ages and other peoples as 'pre-scientific'. It would condemn no rival theory, however seemingly magical and absurd, without studying it. It would not think of primitive peoples as 'lost in a maze of confusion'. It would not use the words 'scientific' and 'unscientific' as if they meant 'Hurrah!' and 'Boo!'

Feyerabend is at variance with Kuhn on a number of points. Kuhn after all believes that scientific training can be carried out only if the student's mind is closed off to everything judged unproductive by his teachers, and that science itself (normal science) can usually be carried out only by people whose minds are closed off against novel theories. On the other hand these two philosophers are not seriously in conflict on other issues. The seeming differences between their views can mostly be explained by the fact that Kuhn discusses two kinds of scientific enterprise, and concentrates on one, namely normal science, whereas Feyerabend is interested mainly in innovative or 'revolutionary' science.

As it turned out, Feyerabend's philosophical pluralism was interpreted by some reviewers of his book *Against Method* as a sign of a deep hostility towards science and scientists, and he was accused without further ado of trying to promote voodoo and astrology. Being evidently a somewhat excitable individual he responded in a polemical fashion with an entertainingly abusive book *Science in a Free Society*. In this work Feyerabend says that in spite of the glowing references which scientists write for themselves and for their profession, and in spite of the prestige they are accorded in the modern world, most real-life scientists are arrogant, pompous, chauvinistic, inhumane, ignorant about everything outside their special subjects, culpably ignorant of the history of science and too stupid and humourless to understand Feyerabend's jokes. Scientists are greatly in need of the intellectual checks which would be provided by an open attitude towards the pluralities of explanation. Feyerabend advises that the best way to instil better attitudes in arrogant scientists would be to bring their activities and salaries under stringent political control (democratic political control, of course).

To consider Feyerabend's political views in detail would take us too far from our topic. Let us end by simply noting that he is one of the few philosophers of our time who sees necessary pluralisms in knowledge, explanation and understanding (Wittgenstein is another). Even Nagel, as we saw in the last chapter, hankers after the 'unitary theory' which he believes might appear many centuries from now.

10

The Study of Mankind

The philosphy of mind is part of the study of mankind. It is an a priori study which however must take some account of what is known about mankind as a species. What is known about mankind includes (*inter alia*) the knowledge that goes to make up a number of different sciences and other theoretical enquiries. At present these sciences and enquiries have the appearance of being autonomous, which is to say that they are severally and jointly indicators of the pluralism of explanation.

However some philosophers believe that the autonomy of the sciences, and even of other enquiries, is merely temporary. These philosophers hold that one day, probably quite soon, all the special sciences (which they sometimes refer to as the 'soft' sciences) will be reduced to physics (the 'hard' science).

Autonomy versus Unity

It was argued in chapter 9 that the concept of science is elastic. At its broadest 'science' can mean any intellectual activity whose methods are regarded by its practitioners or by others as successful, as respectable. (Of course what actually makes methods successful and respectable is a very big question.)

In this broad sense of science modern medicine is a science, mathematics is a science, and Marxist economics is a science if we are to believe Marx himself. In this broad sense technology, i.e. the application of theory to practice, the development of techniques, is 'scientific'. In this broad sense some ways of studying history, theology, philology, are more scientific than others.

More narrowly we can think of science as made up of a set of separate disciplines each of which deals with a different aspect of the world. More narrowly still we may think of science as made up only of disciplines which study the physical world. This conception of science excludes enquiries such as pure mathematics and philology, but includes, of course, the study of living things. So physics has to do with the laws of matter, and with forces like magnetism; physiology has to do with animal organisms; botany has to do with plants; and pathology has to do with illnesses and abnormalities.   It is easy to assume that these separate departments of knowledge map on to pre-existing departments in the world and differ one from the other like natural kinds, but in fact the 'kinds' are not wholly natural since they derive in part from university syllabuses and other human compartmentalisings. This thought gives some slight support to the theory that the various seemingly separate sciences will one day be reduced to a unitary body of knowledge which will turn out to be a descendant of present-day physics.

On the other hand, if we look at physics itself we find that the philosophers who have attempted to explicate its character have said very different things about it. The thesis that physics is the fundamental science to which all the other compartments of science will one day be reduced presupposes that we already know exactly what physics is. Kuhn and Feyerabend have shown that this presupposition is rather shaky.

Although the compartmentalising of the sciences is to some extent the result of syllabuses and the like we can still ask whether this compartmentalising rests on real differences. We can ask whether there are branches of empirical enquiry which are in an ultimate sense autonomous. Is science ultimately unitary, or not?

A complete polymath, acquainted with the results and typical procedures of all the sciences, would perhaps be able to give a well reasoned inductive answer to the question of the autonomy of the sciences. Unfortunately there are no polymaths who we can ask to help us because it is no longer possible to become a polymath in one lifetime. And even polymaths could only say that the evidence *today* indicates that science might (or might not) turn out to be unitary.

Those who favour a reductionist or unitarian approach tend to point to the recent past, when physics and chemistry seemed to be about to merge, and then towards the distant future – for the unity of science is after all an ideal, not a reality. They also rely on models of scientific enquiry which have been deeply influenced by logical positivism and which do not seek but rather presuppose an ultimate unity not only of science but of all respectable enquiry whatsoever.

Those who favour pluralism, on the other hand, tend to look firstly at the empirical evidence given by detailed historical examination of past scientific endeavours, and then at present cases. They argue that the historical evidence throws enough doubt on the models of science originating in logical positivism to discredit them almost completely.

Which side one takes on the issue seems to me to depend partly on temperament. Some people are temperamentally attracted to the lush jungles of pluralism, others to the dry and arctic air of reductionism. (The reader will have perceived that I belong by temperament in the pluralist jungle.)

The Study of Mankind

In the remainder of this chapter I shall use the word 'science' not in its very widest sense, but still in one of the rather wider senses, namely, to refer to any systematized body of theoretical knowledge incorporating at least some empirical elements.

The study of mankind involves many such sciences or departments of knowledge, including bio-chemistry, physiology, neuro-physiology and the study of the anatomy and pathology of the human organism; also the social sciences, such as economics, anthropology, sociology and the study of political institutions. In addition it seems right to treat philology as belonging to the study of mankind, for this subject has always formed a part of anthropology.

The reductionist position in regard to the branches of enquiry which make up the study of mankind is that some of them are 'unscientific', because they contain few laws and many descriptions, and that others, though scientific, are not fundamental. Soft or non-fundamental enquiries such as neuro-physiology, economics, ethnography are in some sense scientific because they have laws and theories, but they are not *as* scientific as the hard sciences of physics and chemistry.

Pluralists will retort to reductionists 'Until you can produce at least one convincing and successful reduction of a "non-fundamental" law or theory to a law of physics, then, whether or not reductionism is useful as a principle, or plausible in the question-begging light of Occam's Razor, still, there is no reason to think that it is actually *true.*'

Is there any reason why non-fundamental laws could not be reduced to the laws of physics? This question cannot be answered completely a priori nor off the top of some philosopher's head. We need to know what the laws of the soft sciences look like, we need to consider some real examples.

Laws in Anthropology

Let us take as examples two laws of anthropology explicated by Edmund Leach, showing here, incidentally, the influence of Levi-Strauss:

1 All the non-verbal dimensions of culture are organised in patterned sets which incorporate coded information.
2 All ritual occasions are concerned with movements across social boundaries from one social status to another (rites of passage).

Leach proves 1 and 2 by collecting examples. He also suggests to his readers that they can collect their own examples if they give the matter a little thought.

1 Examples which fall under the first law include the codes implicit in clothing, in the symbolism of colours and in practices of mutilation such as tattooing, circumcision, head-shaving and so on.

Clothes carry codes in all societies. Clothing codes tell us who is a man, who a woman, who a transvestite, who a priest, who is in mourning, who is about to get married, who is about to play football, etc. They also inform us about the degrees of formality required on social occasions. ('White tie and tails' doesn't go with 'bring a bottle and all your friends'.)

Clothing codes are indicators of present status, among other things. Mutilations are codes which signify change of status. Permanent mutilations go with permanent changes of status, while impermanent mutilations go with changes that can be reversed. Leach mentions circumcision, which in some cultures occurs at puberty, and so signifies the irreversible change from childhood to adulthood, as an example of the former. Head-shaving, on the other hand, goes with changes in status which are physically reversible, or regarded as reversible in principle. Thus in some communities head-shaving is used to mark the fact that a man or a woman has joined a religious order.

2 Rites of passage have a three-phase similarity of structure. First the initiate must be separated from his original role; then there is an interval of 'social timelessness'; finally the initiate is brought back into society and aggregated to his new role.

Separation from the old role is marked by the initiate's moving in procession, or by his removing the clothing proper to the old status, or by the removal of surface dirt by shaving or cleansing, or by mutilation (see above), or by the real or symbolic sacrifice of sacrificial victims. Examples: processions of novitiates up to the altar; the washing of the body of a newly born or newly dead person.

The period of social timelessness may last for a few minutes or for much longer. It is marked by food restrictions or by special clothing or by distancing oneself from normal society by travel or segregation. Examples: the honeymoon; certain phases of some graduation ceremonies; fasting before taking certain sacraments.

The rites of aggregation are similar to the rites of separation. Often they are the same procedures carried out in reverse. Thus processions move in the opposite direction; the special costume worn during the 'timeless' state is removed and the costume of the new status put on; sacrifices are repeated, shaved hair is allowed to grow, food restrictions are removed and so on. Examples: the procession of newly priested men away from the altar; the return of married couples from a special place (the honeymoon venue) to the new home.

Rituals are interval markers in the progression of social time. They mark off phases in the social life of the individual. They are concerned with birth and death, which is movement into and out of life, and with the social movements from single to married, child to adult, sinful to sinless, lay person to religious and so on. All communities and all religions provide instances of this anthropological law.

Possible and Impossible Mapping

Could anthropological laws conceivably turn out to reduce to the laws that govern the behaviour of the particles of particle physics?

It seems clear that reduction is a possibility only if we are able in principle to 'map' the predicates and the logical structures typical of the laws and theories of one science (or one branch of science) on to those typical of another. Otherwise surely the explanatory power of the laws and theories of the 'reduced' science will be lost.

Here is an example of successful mapping, taken from two very soft sciences.

The technical language of professional nutritionists ('vitamins', 'calories', 'trace elements', 'fibre', 'protein', etc.) can be fairly easily mapped on to ordinary descriptions of cookery and meals ('roast beef with green peas and potatoes', 'fried pork with bean sprouts'). Hence statements about specimen meals can in theory be inferred from statements about vitamins, etc., and statements about vitamins, etc., from statements about particular meals. Furthermore, Hempelian laws and theories about nutrition are (in principle, and *ceteris paribus*) stateable both in the language of professional nutritionists and in ordinary language. Kuhnian normal scientists working on jig-saw research probems in nutrition will set out their findings in the language of vitamins and calories, but they can expect those findings to be translated into catering decisions expressed in the language of cookery.

Roughly speaking, many predicates proper to the science of nutrition are co-extensive with predicates proper to the science of cookery.

Now a different kind of example. Vulgar fractions and decimal fractions cannot be mapped on to one another, for although there is a decimal fraction for every vulgar fraction the converse is of course not the case. This is the irreducible pluralism, occurring inside a single 'science', which worried the Pythagoreans. But it no longer worries either scientists or philosophers, even reductionist philosophers. Why not? Maybe just because it does occur within a single 'science', and a respectable science at that. (Readers who do not agree with this explanation are invited to think up a better one.)

Properties and Bridge Laws

A reduction of the laws of one science to those of another requires the following:

1 The properties and predicates proper to the first science must be ultimately co-extensive with the properties and predicates proper to the second.
2 There must be true bridge laws linking the laws of the two sciences.
3 The bridge laws must express relationships which are both transitive and symmetrical.

1 Every science contains a taxonomy of the things, events and states which make up its own area or special universe of discourse. Every science therefore has a vocabulary of predicates many of which are special to that particular science. The descriptions made with these predicates form the premises in the reasoning that make up the inferences and inference patterns which constitute the laws and discoveries of the science in question.

For reduction of some one science to physics to be possible the predicates proper to that science must be co-extensive with predicates (or sets of predicates) proper to physics.

We need to bear in mind that not every true description of an event is a description in the vocabulary of a science. For instance, as Jerry Fodor remarks, the description of events as 'such-and-such a thing being taken to within 3 miles of the Eiffel Tower' is not part of a science. There is no natural law which applies to events in virtue of their instantiating this description. The property *is being taken* . . . is not a natural kind and the description 'is being taken . . .' is not a natural kind predicate. The debate as to whether reductionism is true or not is not concerned with accidental truths along the lines of something's being three miles from the Eiffel Tower and such: it is concerned with natural kinds and with causal laws and with properties and predicates proper to scientific enquiry.

2 It is generally agreed that the reduction of one science to another must involve bridge laws. Bridge laws contain predicates from two sciences. Hence, for instance, in order for a law of chemistry to be reducible to a law of physics it is necessary that predicates from both sciences appear in the relevant bridge laws.

The schema of a reduction law (between physics and chemistry, say) may be represented as follows:

Let P_1 and P_2 be predicates of physics.
Let C_1 and C_2 be predicates of chemistry.
(*Ex hypothesi*, C_1, C_2, P_1 and P_2 are natural kind predicates.)

Let formula (1) represent an inference based on a law of chemistry:

$$C1.x \rightarrow C2.y. \tag{1}$$

This is to be read initially as 'For very event consisting of x being C1 we may infer that there is an event consisting of y being C2.'

Let formula (3) represent an inference based on a law of physics:

$$P1.x \rightarrow P2.y. \tag{3}$$

This is to be read initially as 'For every event of x being P1 we may infer that there is an event of y being P2.'

Let the formulae (2a) and (2b) represent inferences corresponding to a bridge law:

$$C1.x \longleftrightarrow P1.x. \tag{2a}$$
$$C2.y \longleftrightarrow P2.y. \tag{2b}$$

Formula (2a) is to be read initially as 'For every event consisting of x being C1 we may infer that there is an event of x being P1' and (2b) as 'For every event consisting of y being C2 we may infer that there is an event of y being P2.'

3 Bridge laws, essential to reduction, themselves presuppose that the properties and predicates of one science can correspond to the properties and predicates, or to conjunctive sets of these, of another. They also presuppose the validity of the notion of contingent identity.

It can be seen that bridge laws linking sciences must express relations which are both transitive and symmetrical. If anthropology (for instance) could be reduced to physics this would have to happen via a reduction to psychology, then to neurology, then to biochemistry, then to physics. It follows that there will be a largish number of true bridge laws, since there will need to be at least one bridge law for each pair of laws from every pair of sciences in the reductive series.

The schema of such a reductive series can be represented as follows:

$$A1.x \longrightarrow A2.y. \tag{1}$$
$$A1.x \longleftrightarrow Ps1.x. \tag{2a}$$
$$A2.y \longleftrightarrow Ps2.y. \tag{2b}$$
$$Ps1.x \longleftrightarrow N1.x. \tag{3a}$$
$$Ps2.y \longleftrightarrow N2.y \tag{3b}$$
$$N1.x \longleftrightarrow B1.x. \tag{4a}$$
$$N2.y \longleftrightarrow B2.y. \tag{4b}$$

$$B1.x \longleftrightarrow P1.x. \qquad (5a)$$
$$B2.y \longleftrightarrow P2.y. \qquad (5b)$$
$$P1.x \longrightarrow P2.y. \qquad (6)$$

where A1,2 represent terms in anthropology, Ps1,2 terms in psychology, N1,2 terms in neurology, B1,2 terms in biochemistry and P1,2 terms in physics, and where (2a,b) and (3a,b) and (4a,b) and (5a,b) all represent inferences based on bridge laws.

As to (1) and (6), they represent inferences based on laws in anthropology and physics respectively of course.

What justifies the inferences represented by $\rightarrow$ and by $\longleftrightarrow$?

Since in reducing anthropology (say) to physics there has to be more than one bridge law, the connectives $\rightarrow$ and $\longleftrightarrow$ will have to represent transitive relations. Furthermore the connective $\longleftrightarrow$ will have to represent a symmetrical relation.

If the relations expressed by the bridge laws are not transitive, then the reduction will fail at the point at which the relation expressed by $\longleftrightarrow$ fails to carry through. If the relations expressed by the bridge laws are not symmetrical then physics will merely be *linked* or *connected* to the other science, and will not be its fundamental basis.

Suppose we read $\rightarrow$ as 'brings about' or 'causes' and agree for the sake of argument that causation is a transitive relation.

How are we to read the connective $\longleftrightarrow$? Causation is asymmetrical whereas bridge laws must express symmetrical relations.

It seems that the best way to read the bridge law connective $\longleftrightarrow$ is as asserting contingent identity, for genuine identity of course is transitive and symmetrical.

If the connective is read in that way then, if reductionism *per se* is true, it will follow that all the predicates proper to any one science will each of them be co-extensive with a predicate or conjunction of predicates in every other science. This seems prima facie improbable, but let us accept it for the sake of argument.

Furthermore, contingent identity itself is a problematic notion, as we saw in chapter 2. But let's for the sake of argument ignore those problems too.

There now emerges a new problem which is recognised even by some would-be reductionists – by Jerry Fodor for example.

The problem is this: it seems very evident that any identity that may hold between properties in a soft and a hard science, respectively, will hold not between single soft properties and single hard properties, and not between single soft properties and conjunctions of hard properties, but between soft properties and DISJUNCTIONS of hard properties.

Now, a disjunction is not a true property.

To take an earlier example, it seems plain on reflection that if any properties and predicates proper to physics correspond to the anthropological property of *being a ritual* the correspondence must be by way of disjunction. For rituals are so immensely various that they could not possibly have in common any single physical property or conjunction of properties, even at a macro level, let alone at the level of particle physics. Even on the most optimistic assumptions (from the point of view of a reductionist that is) the property of being a ritual will only turn out to be contingently identical with a disjunction of psychological properties, each of which will be contingently identical with a disjunction of neuro-physiological properties, each of which will be contingently identical with a disjunction of bio-chemical properties, each of which might be contingently identical with a conjunction or disjunction of properties belonging to the particles of particle physics.

Thus what corresponds, in physics, to the anthropological property can only be an absolutely enormous disjunction of 'physical particle properties'. What corresponds, among the atoms and electrons, to the property of *being a ritual* can only be a vastly huge disjunction of events and properties of the kinds describable in terms proper to physics, reached too only via other enormous disjunctions of psychological, physiological (etc.) properties.

For this reason the logical positivists' theory that all science can be reduced to physics seems to me to be rather less reliable than a pipe dream.

However not all reductionists are committed to physics. Thomas Nagel for instance, as we saw in chapter 8, is a short-term pluralist and a long-term monist who does not hold that physics is the ultimate science. His suggestion that one day, hundreds of years from now, a new science might emerge which will be capable of giving a completely unified account of the world and our experience of it does not entail any commitment to physics as such.

I see no overwhelming reason why Nagel's prophecy might not prove true and no overwhelming reason why it might not prove false. In my view the truth of monism and the falsehood of pluralism is logically possible, and the falsehood of monism and the truth of pluralism is also logically possible. At present it would be mere dogmatism to claim to know for certain that monism, or pluralism, is true.

Appendix
Authors Referred to in this Book

(Authors are listed in reverse alphabetical order.)

LUDWIG WITTGENSTEIN: Austrian/British philosopher, born in Vienna in 1889, died in Cambridge in 1951. Wittgenstein studied engineering in Germany and Manchester, and in about 1911 went to Cambridge in order to meet Bertrand Russell. He wrote his first book, the *Tractatus Logico-Philosophicus,* as a POW in Italy in the First World War and Russell helped him to find a publisher. His other writings were published only after his death. He was professor of philosophy in Cambridge between 1939 and 1947/8.

J.B. WATSON: American psychologist, born 1878, died 1958, generally regarded as the founder of behaviourism. His PhD thesis was an investigation into the behaviour of the rat. Watson taught in Johns Hopkins University until 1920 when he resigned and started a new career in advertising.

ALAN TURING: British mathematician and logician, born in India in 1912, died in England in 1954. Turing studied mathematics at Cambridge in the 1930s and attended some of Wittgenstein's lectures in 1939. He worked in mathematical research in Cambridge, Princeton and Manchester, writing important essays on foundational topics and a seminal paper in *Mind* (1950) on artificial intelligence. During the Second World War he did highly important work as a code-breaker.

P.F. STRAWSON: British philosopher, Wayneflete professor of philosophy in the University of Oxford.

TIMOTHY SPRIGGE: Professor of philosophy in the University of Edinburgh.

J.J.C. SMART: British/Australian philosopher, born in Cambridge in 1920, appointed professor of philosophy in the University of Adelaide in 1950. Smart is arguably the most distinguished exponent of physicalism, also known as the mind/brain identity theory. He studied philosophy in Oxford under the supervision of Ryle and for a time regarded himself as a philosophical behaviourist.

B.F. SKINNER: American psychologist, born in 1904. Radical behaviourist, inventor of techniques and devices for investigating the behaviour of laboratory animals, including the so-called 'Skinner Box'. He is the author of many technical works in psychology and a Utopia novel, *Walden II*.

JOHN SEARLE: American philosopher, born in 1933, educated in America and Oxford, author of *Speech Acts* and *Intentionality*, professor of philosophy in the University of California.

OLIVER SACKS: British neurologist, born in England in 1933. Dr Sacks works in America with geriatric patients and has carried out research into the 1920s sleeping sickness epidemic and its long-term results. He is also a successful author.

GILBERT RYLE: British philosopher, born in Brighton in 1900, died in Oxford in 1976. Author of *The Concept of Mind* and *Dilemmas*, editor for many years of the journal *Mind*, Wayneflete professor of philosophy in the University of Oxford.

RICHARD RORTY: American philosopher, professor of philosophy in the University of Virginia.

HILARY PUTNAM: American philosopher, author of *Mind, Language and Reality* and several other collections of essays, professor of philosophy at Harvard University.

THOMAS NAGEL: American philosopher, born in Yugoslavia in 1937. Nagel migrated to the USA at the age of one, studied in Cornell, Harvard and Oxford; he is author of *The Possibility of Altruism* and *The View from Nowhere*, and professor of philosophy at New York University.

G.E. MOORE: British philosopher, born 1873, died 1958, professor of philosophy at Cambridge 1925–39.

MAURICE MERLEAU-PONTY: French philosopher and man of letters, born in 1908, Merleau-Ponty lectured at the Sorbonne and was a literary colleague of J.P. Sartre. He is regarded as one of the most original exponents of the philosophy of phenomenology. He died in 1961.

D.H. MELLOR: British philosopher, born in 1938, professor of philosophy in the University of Cambridge.

DAVID LEWIS: American philosopher who works and publishes in both America and Australia. Lewis is the inventor of modal realism or the 'possible worlds' theory.

CLAUDE LEVI-STRAUSS: French anthropologist and philosopher, born in Belgium in 1908. Levi-Strauss studied in Paris, became professor of sociology in Sao Paulo, undertook ethnographic fieldwork in the interior of Brazil, and served as French Cultural Attache in the USA in 1946/7. He is the author of many books illustrating structuralist principles of explanation.

EDMUND LEACH: British anthropologist, born in 1910. Leach undertook ethnographic field research in Burma, Formosa (Taiwan) and Ceylon (Sri Lanka) and is the author of many works on anthropology. He was Provost of King's College Cambridge between 1972 and 1978.

THOMAS KUHN: American philosopher of science, author of *The Structure of Scientific Revolutions*.

SAUL KRIPKE: American mathematician and philosopher, born in 1940, professor of philosophy at Princeton University.

CARL HEMPEL: German/American philosopher of science associated with the Vienna school. He was born in 1905, left Nazi Germany in 1934 moving first to Brussels and then to the USA. He set out his theory.of scientific explanation in 1948, revising it in 1962.

ERNEST GELLNER: British sociologist, author of (*inter alia*) a well-known attack on Oxford linguistic philosophy called *Words and Things*.

JERRY FODOR: American professor of philosophy at the Graduate Center, City University of New York.

PAUL FEYERABEND: Austrian/American philosopher, educated in Vienna, Weimar, Alpbach and London. Feyerabend invented a type of philosophy described by him as epistemological anarchism or epistemological dada-ism.

DONALD DAVIDSON: American philosopher, born in 1917, author of *Actions and Events* and *The Logic of Grammar*, former professor of philosophy at the University of Chicago.

RUDOLF CARNAP: German/American philosopher, born in Germany in 1891, died in America in 1970. He taught in Vienna, Prague, Chicago and California, was a central member of the Vienna Circle, or logical positivist school of philosophy.

NED BLOCK: American professor of philosophy at the Massachusetts Institute of Technology.

D.M. ARMSTRONG: Australian philosopher, born in 1926. He studied at the Universities of Sydney, Oxford and Melbourne, and is Challis professor of philosophy in the University of Sydney.

Bibliography
by Chapters

Chapter 1 Behaviourism

B.F. Skinner, *Science and Human Behavior*, New York, 1953.
B.F. Skinner, *Beyond Freedom and Dignity*, London, 1972.
B.F. Skinner, *Reflections on Behaviorism and Society*, Baltimore, 1978.
J.B. Watson, *Psychology from a Behaviorist Standpoint*, Baltimore, 1919.

Chapter 2 Physicalism

Saul Kripke, *Naming and Necessity*, Amsterdam, 1972/ Oxford, 1980.
J.J.C. Smart, 'Sensations and brain processes', *The Philosophical Review*, 1959.
J.J.C. Smart, *Philosophy & Scientific Realism*, London, 1969.

Chapter 3 Functionalism

D.M. Armstrong, 'The Nature of Mind', Inaugural Lecture 1965, in Ned Block (ed.), *Papers in the Philosophy of Psychology*, 1985.
Ned Block, 'Problems with functionalism', in Block, *Papers*, op. cit.
David Lewis, 'Mad pain and Martian pain', in Block, *Papers*, op. cit.
John Searle, 'Minds brains and programs', in J. Haugeland (ed.), *Mind Design*, Cambridge, Mass., 1981.
Alan Turing, 'Computers and intelligence', in *Mind*, 1950.
Alan Turing, 'Intelligent machinery', in B. Melzer and D. Michie (eds), *Machine Intelligence*, Edinburgh, 1969.

Chapter 4 Language and Forms of Life: Wittgenstein

L. Wittgenstein, *Philosophical Investigations*, translated by G.E.M. Anscombe, Oxford, 1953.

L. Wittgenstein, *The Blue and Brown Books*, Oxford, 1958.
L. Wittgenstein, *Zettel*, translated by G.E.M. Anscombe, Oxford, 1967.
L. Wittgenstein, *Culture and Value*, translated by Peter Winch, Oxford, 1980.
L. Wittgenstein, *Letters to C.K. Ogden*, Oxford, 1973.
L. Wittgenstein, *Letters to Russell, Keynes and Moore*, Oxford, 1974.
J.R. Bambrough, 'Universals and family resemblances', *Proceedings of the Aristotelian Society*, 1960–1.
Ernest Gellner, *Words and Things*, London, 1959.
Norman Malcolm and G.H. von Wright, *Ludwig Wittgenstein: A Memoir*, Oxford, 1966.

Chapter 5 Language and Behaviour: Ryle

Gilbert Ryle, *The Concept of Mind*, London, 1949.
D.M. Armstrong, *Belief Truth & Knowledge*, Cambridge, 1974, chapter 2.

Chapter 6 Body and Mind: Merleau-Ponty

Maurice Merleau-Ponty, *The Phenomenology of Perception*, translated by Colin Smith, London, 1962.
Maurice Merleau-Ponty, *The Visible and the Invisible*, translated by H.F. and P.A. Dreyfus, Evanston, Ill., 1968.

Chapter 7 Structuralism: Levi-Strauss

Claude Levi-Strauss, *Totemism*, London, 1964.
Claude Levi-Strauss, *The Savage Mind*, London, 1966.
Claude Levi-Strauss, *The Raw and the Cooked*, London, 1970.
Sigmund Freud, *Totem and Taboo* (Penguin edn).
Edmund Leach, *Levi-Strauss*, London, 1970.

Chapter 8 Varieties of Dualism

Donald Davidson, 'Mental Events', in his *Actions and Events*, Oxford, 1980.
T. Nagel, 'What is it like to be a bat?' *Philosophical Review*, 1974.
T. Nagel, *The View from Nowhere*, Oxford, 1986.
Hilary Putnam, 'The meaning of "meaning"', in his *Mind, Language and Reality*, Cambridge, 1975. (See esp. p. 220, on methodological solipsism.)
Richard Rorty, 'Mind-body identity, privacy and categories', in *Philosophy of Mind* (ed. Stuart Hampshire), New York, 1966.

Timothy Sprigge, 'Final Causes', in *Proceedings of the Aristotelian Society*, Supplementary Volume, 1971.

Oliver Sacks, 'Reminiscences', in *The Man who Mistook his Wife for a Hat*, London, 1984.

Chapter 9   *The Study of Matter and its Laws*

Paul Feyerabend, *Against Method*, London, 1975.

Paul Feyerabend, *Science in a Free Society*, London, 1978.

Carl Hempel, 'Rational Action', in his *Aspects of Scientific Explanation*, New York, 1965.

Thomas Kuhn, *The Structure of Scientific Revolutions*, Chicago, 1962.

Chapter 10   *The Study of Mankind*

Jerry Fodor, *The Language of Thought*, Brighton, Sussex, 1976.

Arnold van Gennep, *The Rites of Passage*, translated by M.B. Vizedom and G.L. Caffee, London, 1960; originally published in France as *Rites du passage* in 1908.

Edmund Leach, *Culture and Communication*, Cambridge, 1976, chapters 13, 17.

Additional Bibliography

D.M. Armstrong, *A Materialist Theory of Mind*, London, 1968.
John Aubrey, *Brief Lives* (life of Hooke).
A.J. Ayer, *Philosophy in the Twentieth Century*, London, 1982.
Ned Block (ed.), *Papers in the Philosophy of Psychology*, London, 1980.
Rudolf Carnap, 'Psychology in physical language', in *Logical Positivism* (ed. A.J. Ayer), Glencoe, Ill., 1959.
Cora Diamond (ed.), *Wittgenstein's Lectures on the Foundations of Mathematics 1939*, Brighton, 1976.
Paul Feyerabend, *Farewell to Reason*, London, 1987.
Alan Hodges, *Alan Turing: The Enigma*, London, 1983.
Saul Kripke, 'Wittgenstein on rules and private language', in *Perspectives on the Philosophy of Wittgenstein* (ed. Irving Block), Oxford, 1981.
Francois H. Lapointe, *Ludwig Wittgenstein: A Comprehensive Bibliography*, New Haven, Conn. and London, 1980.
Claude Levi-Strauss, *The Origin of Table Manners*, translated by John and Doreen Weightman, London, 1978.
David Lewis, *The Plurality of Worlds*, Oxford, 1986.
Maurice Merleau-Ponty, *Sense and Nonsense*, translated by H.F. Dreyfus and P.A. Dreyfus, Evanston, Ill. 1964.
Mary Midgeley, *Science and Religion* (GSM Sermon, 19 October 1986), obtainable from Great St Mary's Church, Cambridge.
W. Penfield and P. Perot, 'The brain's record of visual and auditory experience: a final summary and discussion', in *Brain*, 1963.
Hilary Putnam, 'The nature of mental states', in his *Mind, Language & Reality*, Cambridge, 1975.
Oliver Sacks, *Awakenings*, London, 1973.
John Searle, *Intentionality*, Cambridge, 1983.
B.F. Skinner, *Walden II*, New York and London, 1948.
P.F. Strawson, *Individuals*, London, 1959.
J.B. Watson, *Behavior*, Baltimore, 1914.
L. Wittgenstein, *Remarks on the Philosophy of Psychology*, Oxford, 1980.

Index